MOON FOR THE MISBEGOTTEN?

E.M. SCHORB

HILL HOUSE   NEW YORK

ISBN: 978-0-692-97774-3

This book was made possible by a grant from Robert Rauschenberg and Change, Inc.

Several of these cartoons appeared in *Dates and Dreams, Short Fictions, Prose Poems, Cartoons*, Winner of the Writer's Digest Book Award for Poetry; Honorable Mention at the New York Book Festival; and Finalist in the 2017 Best Book Awards.

With thanks for technical assistance, layout, and design to my wife, Patricia Schorb and my daughter, Selah Bunzey.

for Ludwig Datené

INTRODUCTION

PEOPLE

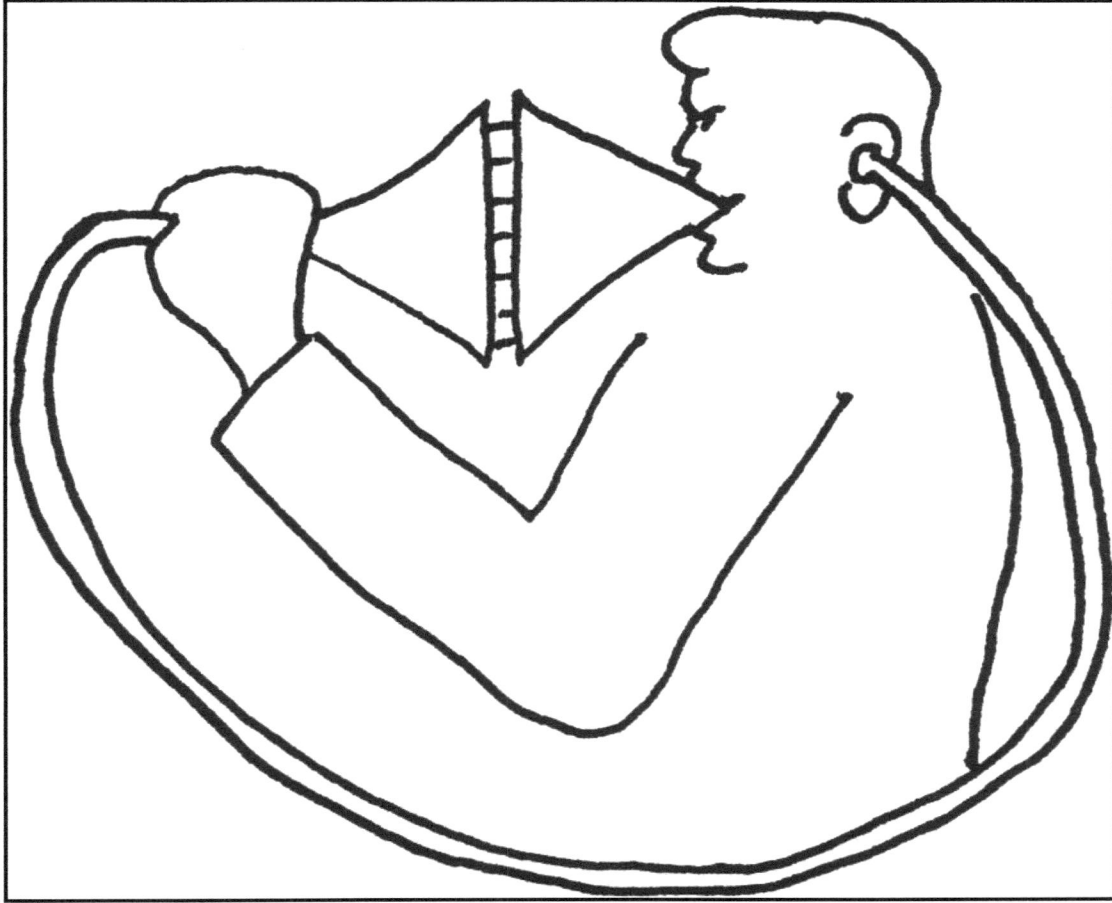

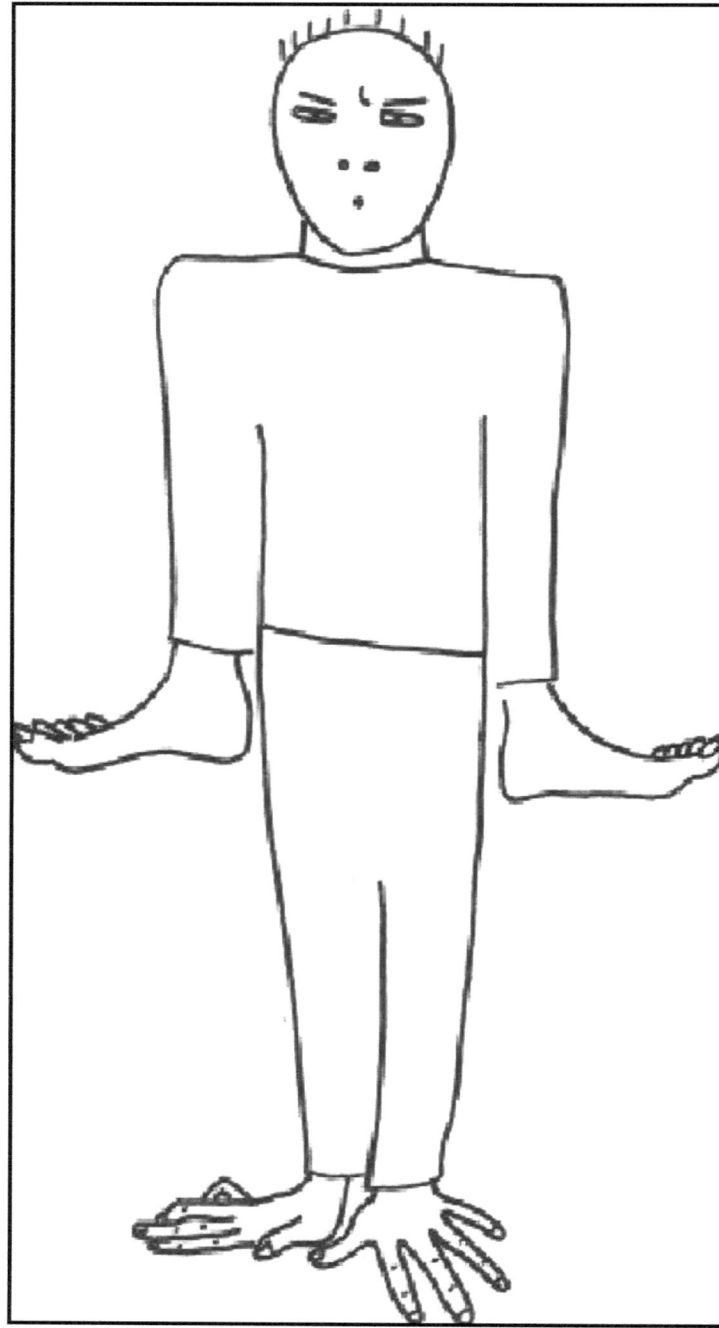

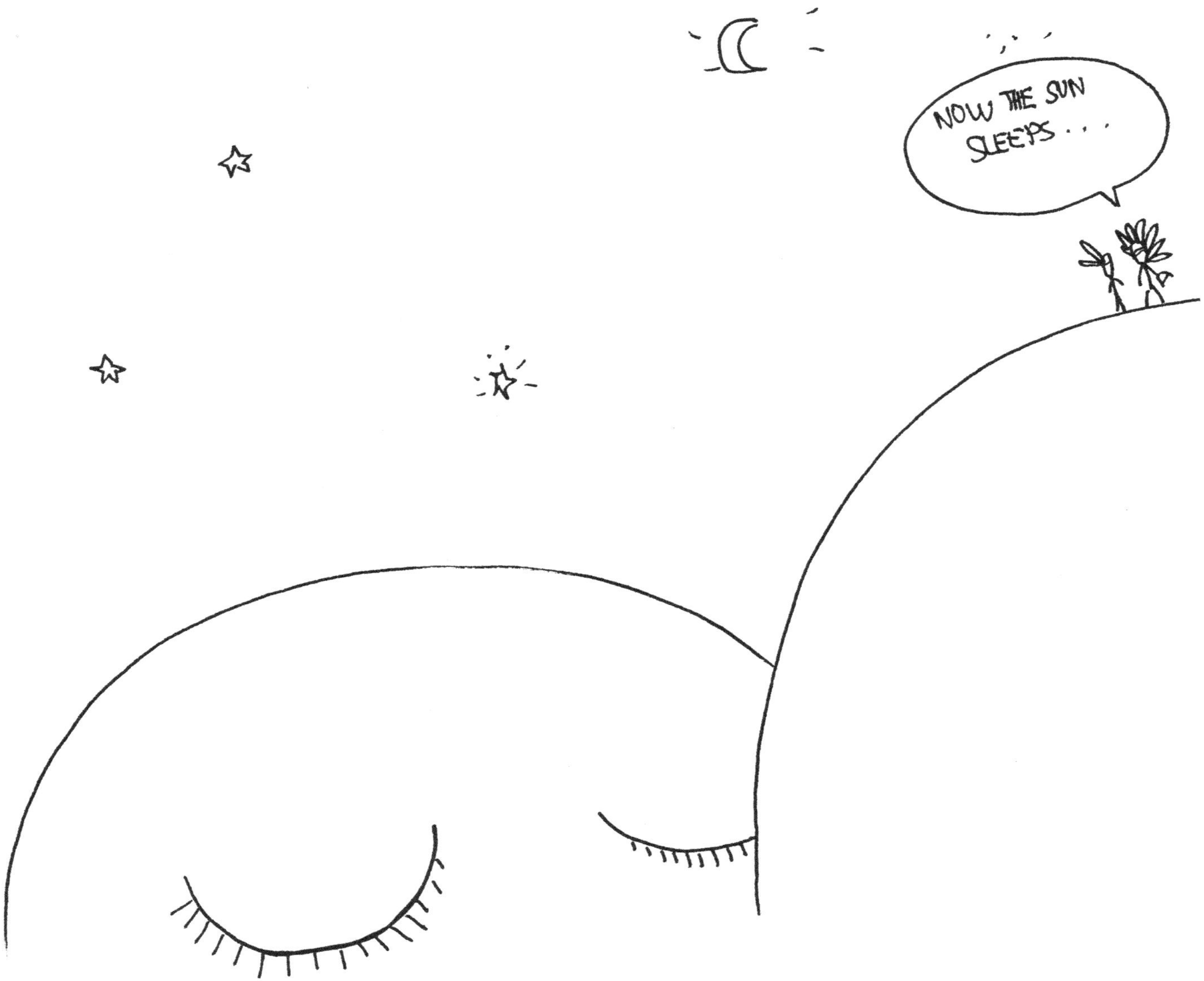
NOW THE SUN SLEEPS . . .

SEE YOU TOMORROW!

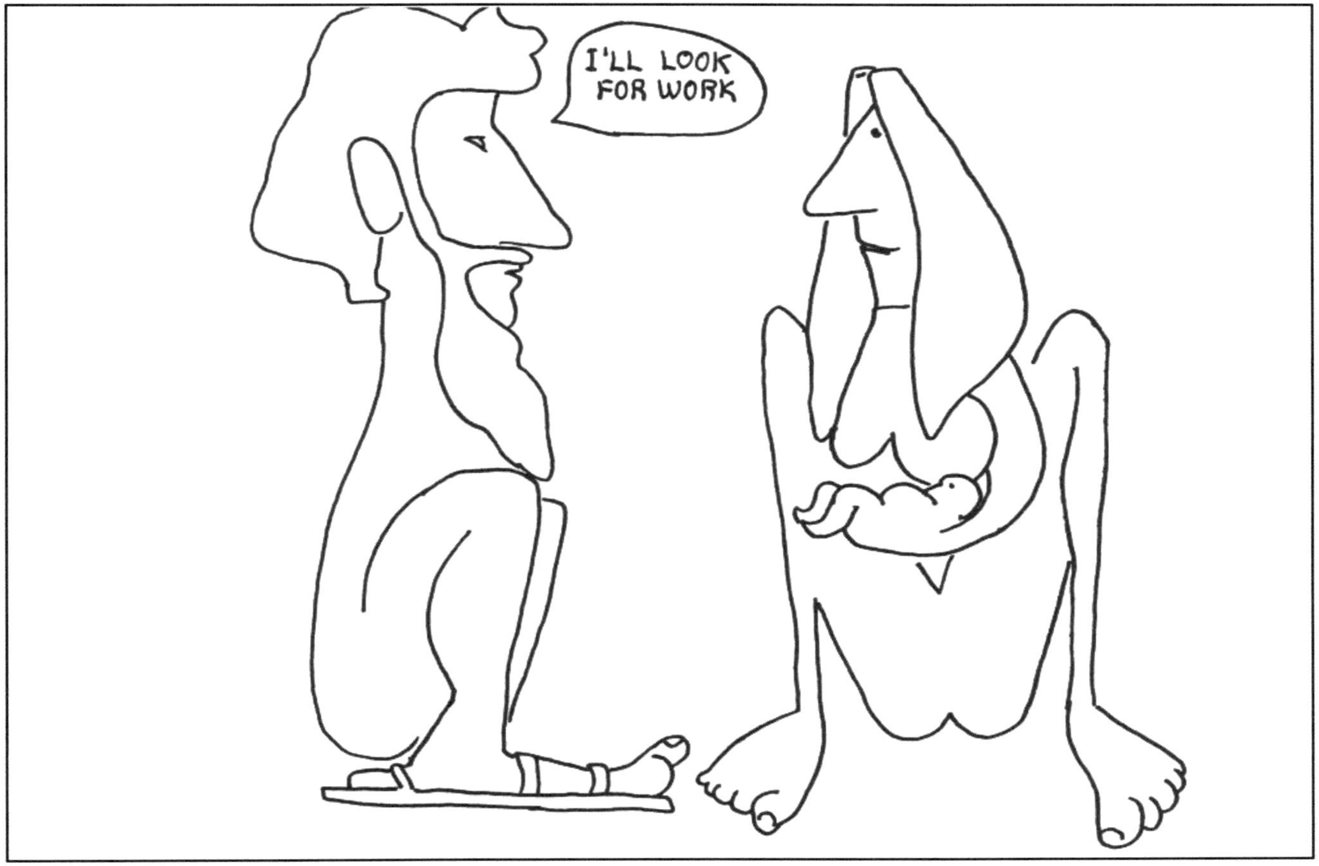
I'LL LOOK FOR WORK

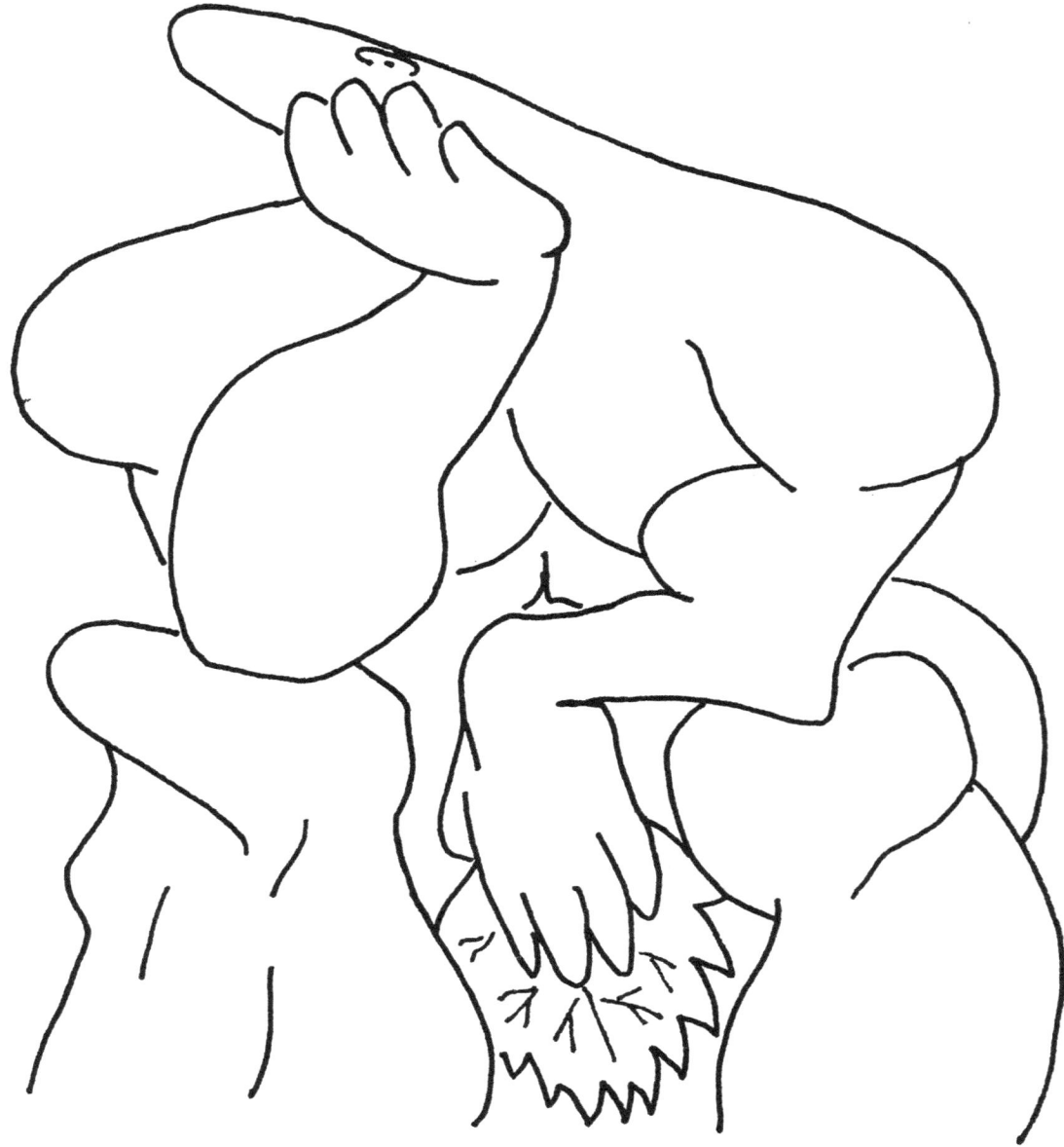

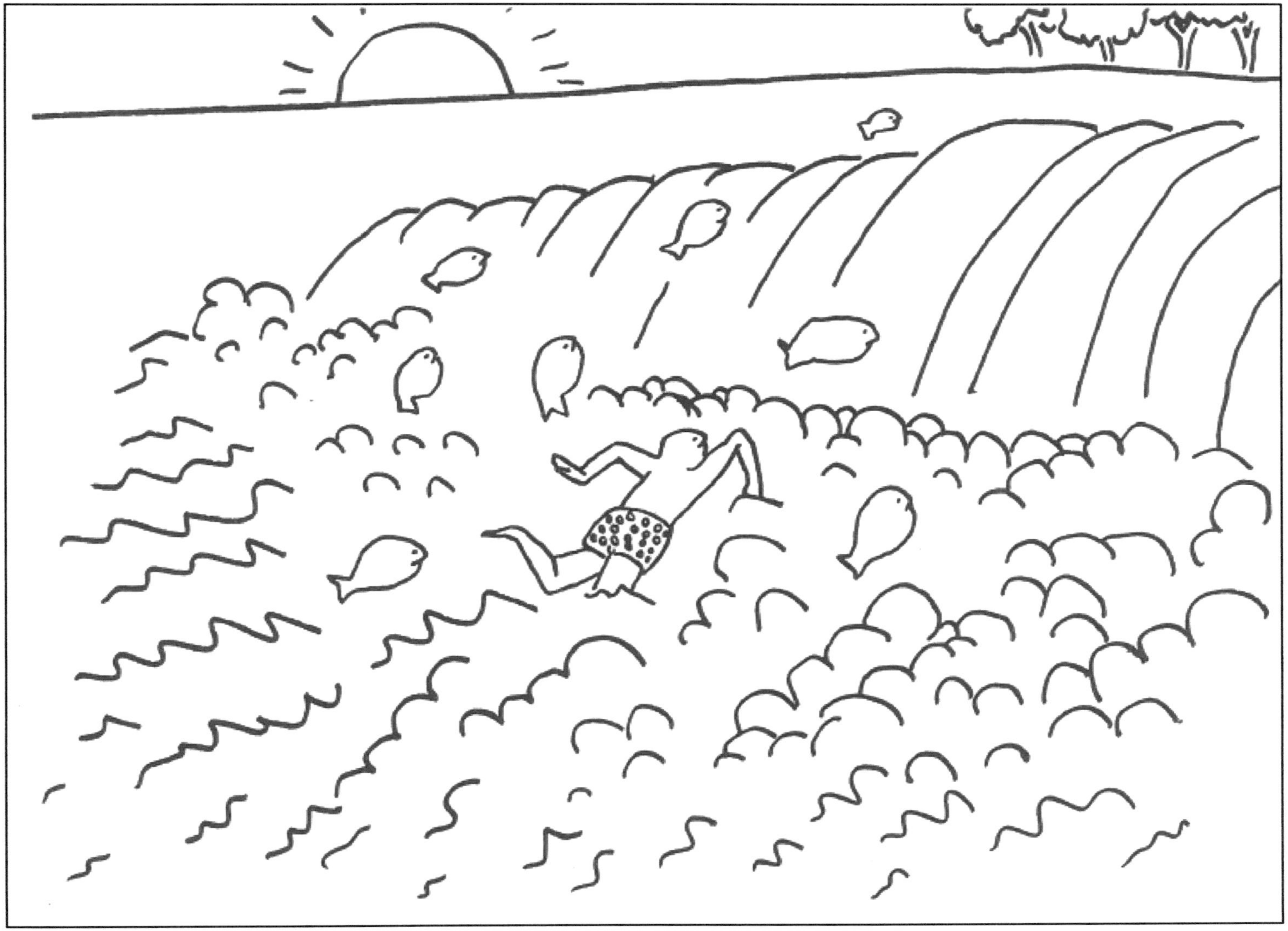

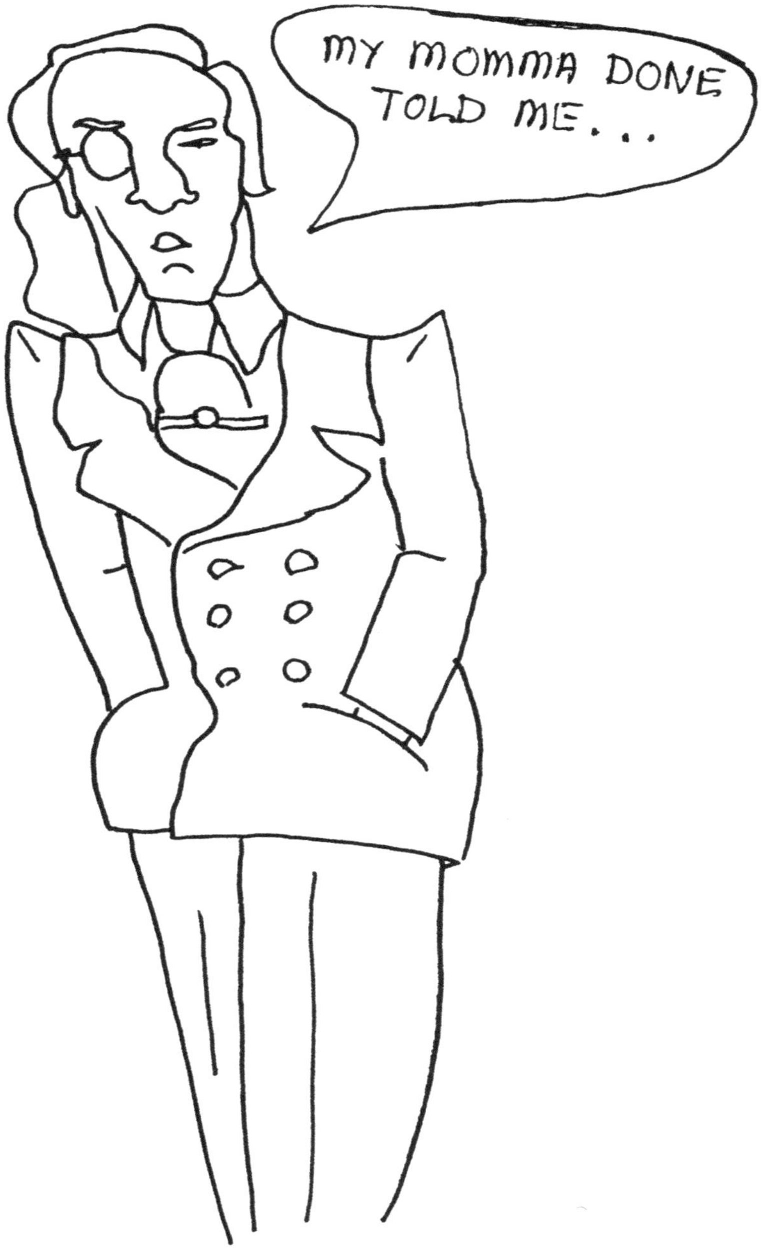
MY MOMMA DONE
TOLD ME...

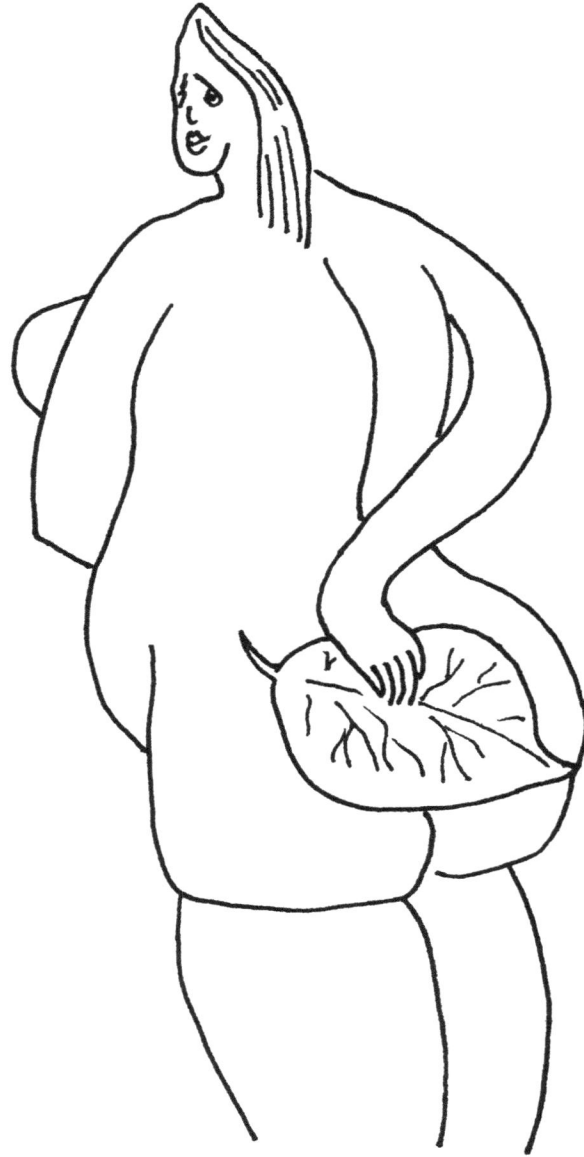

THE LEADER

SHE'S GOT SOMETHING

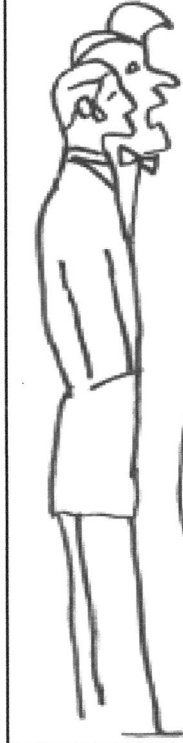

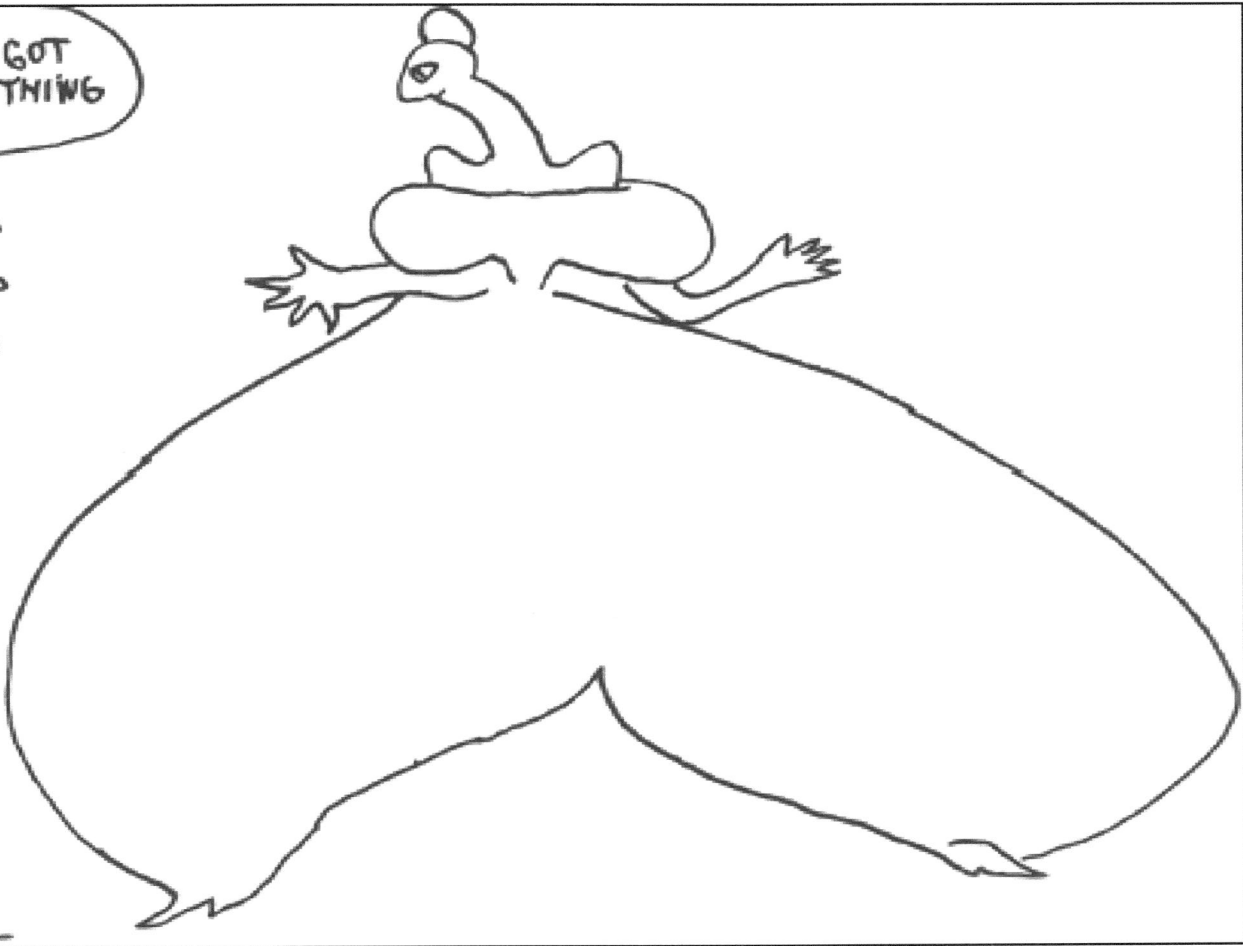

GURU FRAPPÉ

WE'RE GOING STEADY

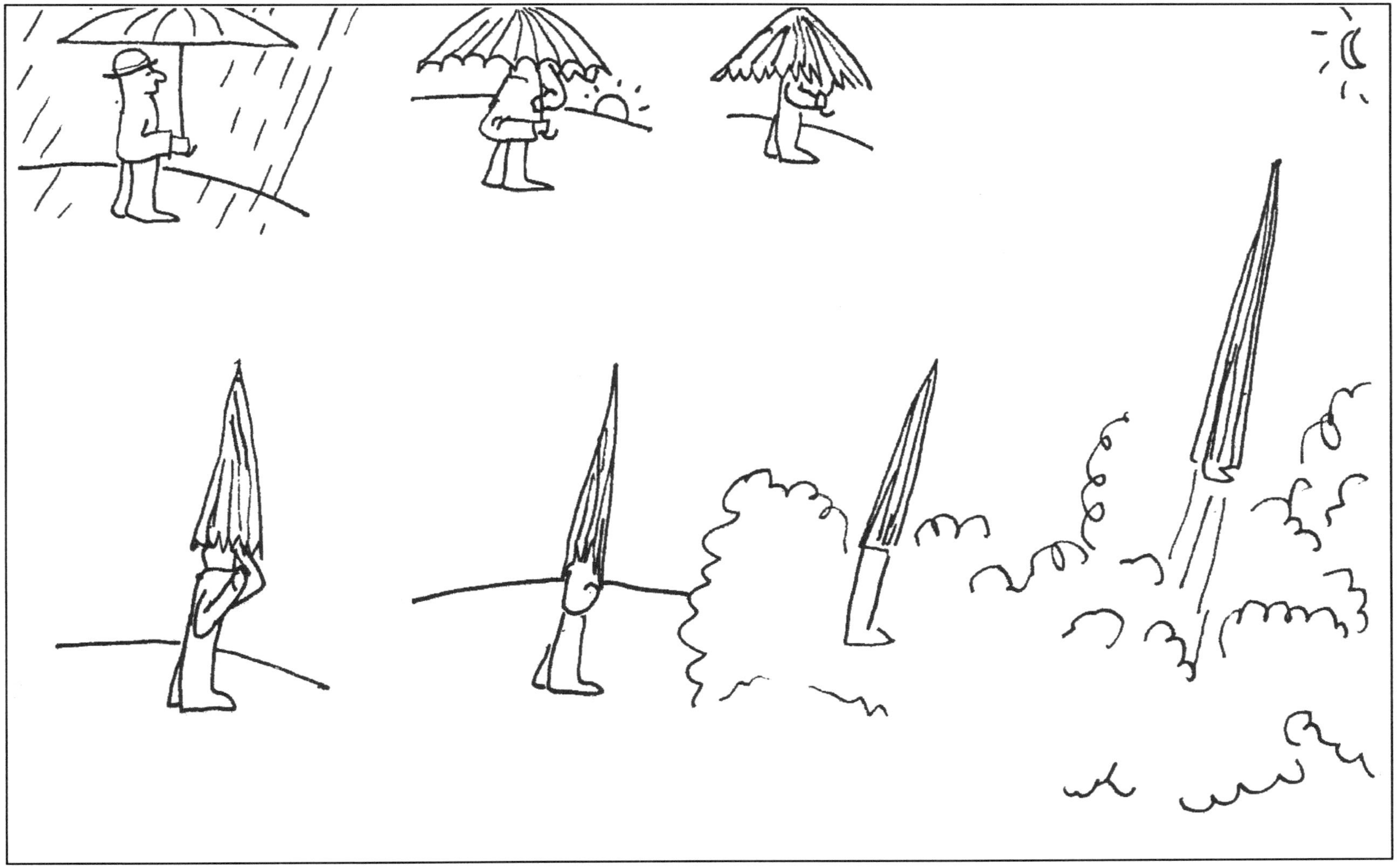

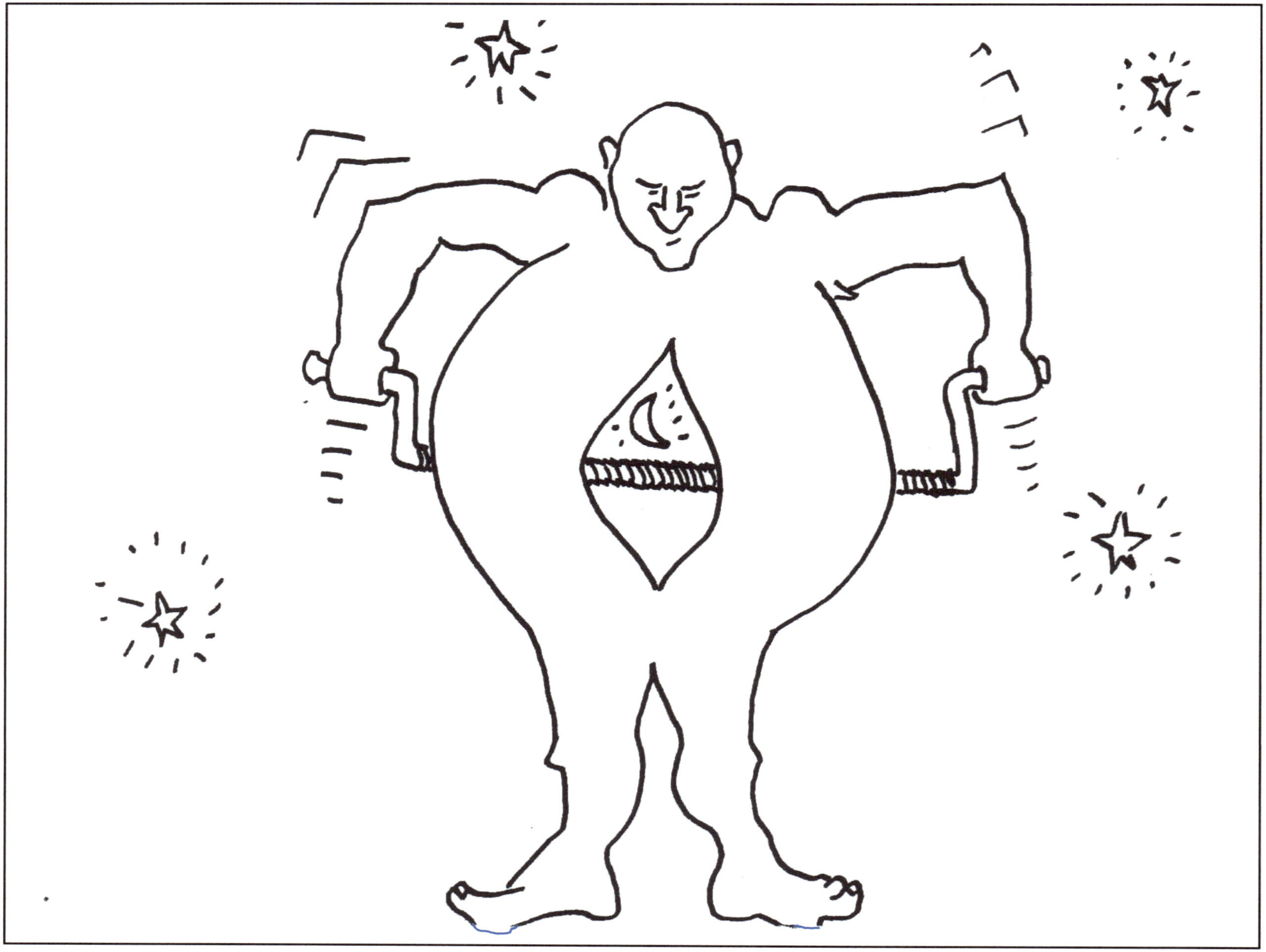

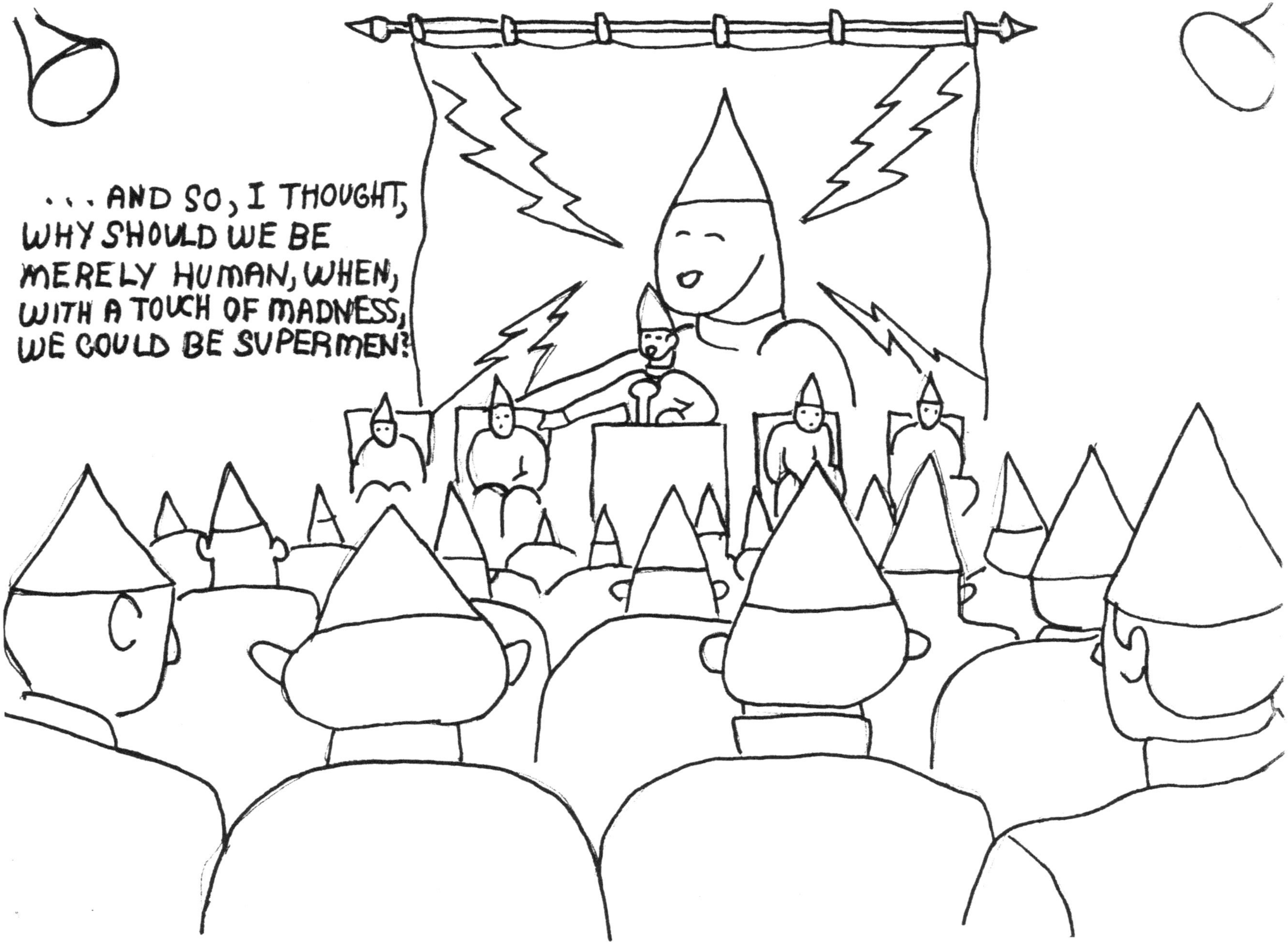
. . . AND SO, I THOUGHT, WHY SHOULD WE BE MERELY HUMAN, WHEN, WITH A TOUCH OF MADNESS, WE COULD BE SUPERMEN?

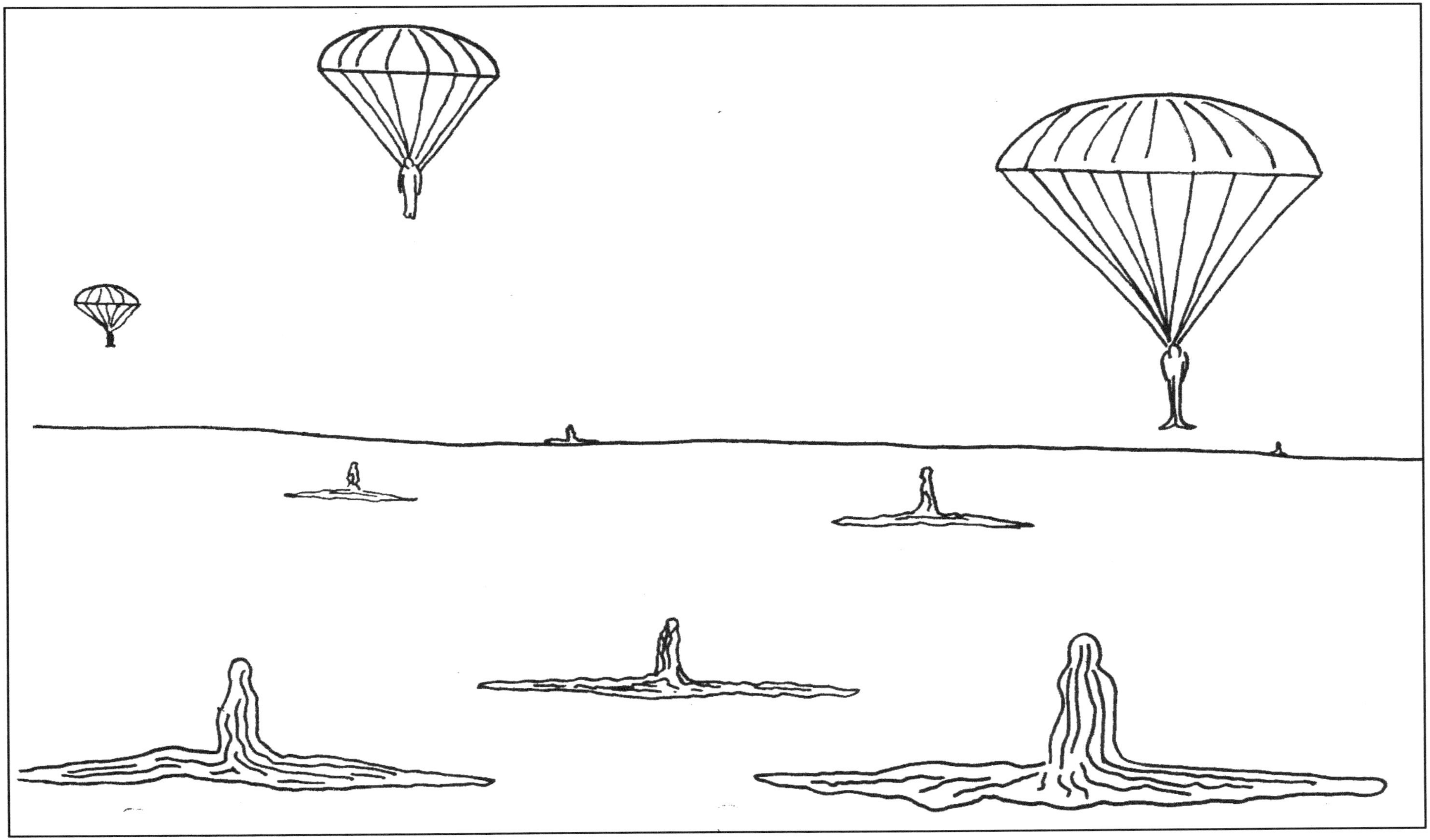

LET ME ENTERTAIN YOU...

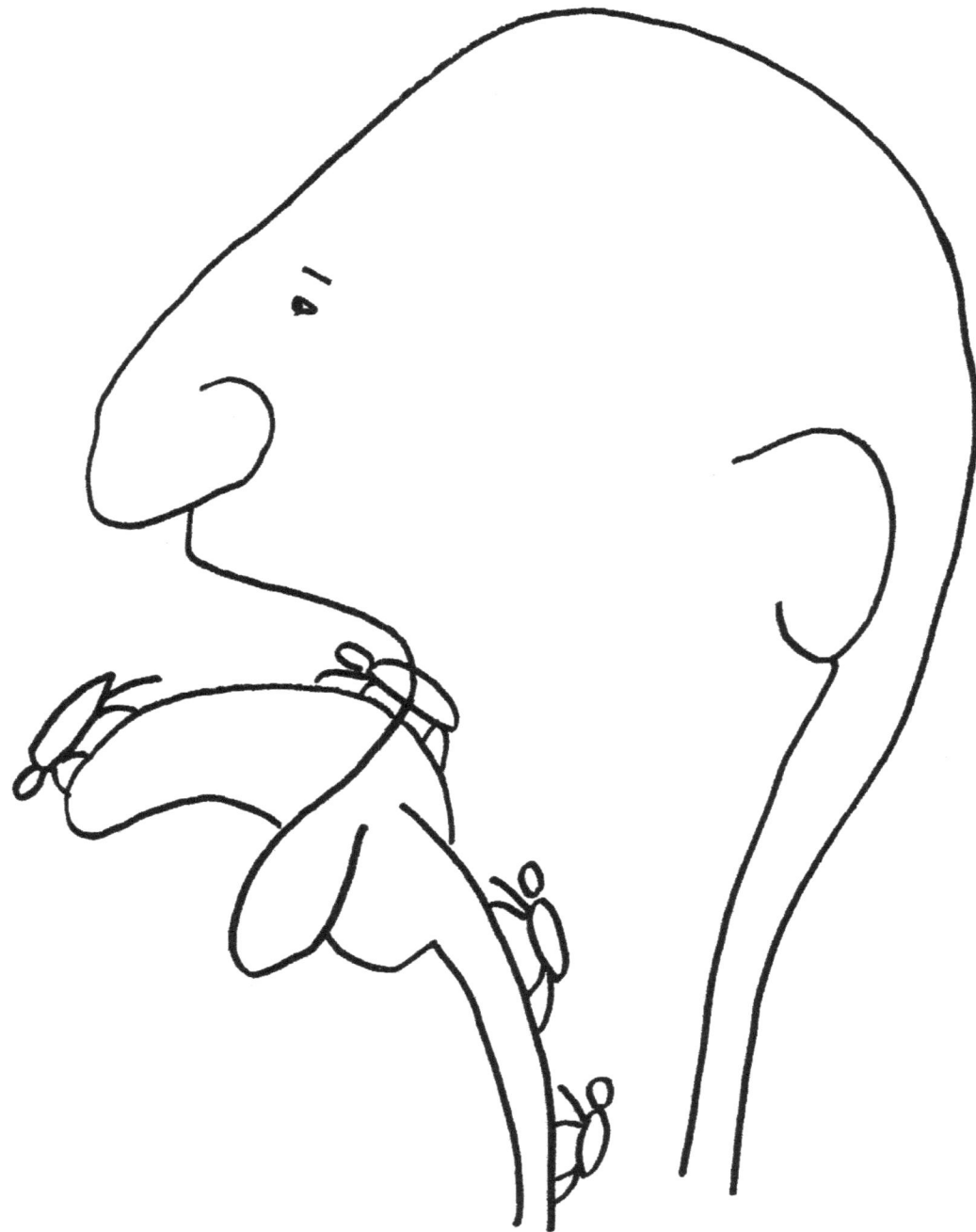

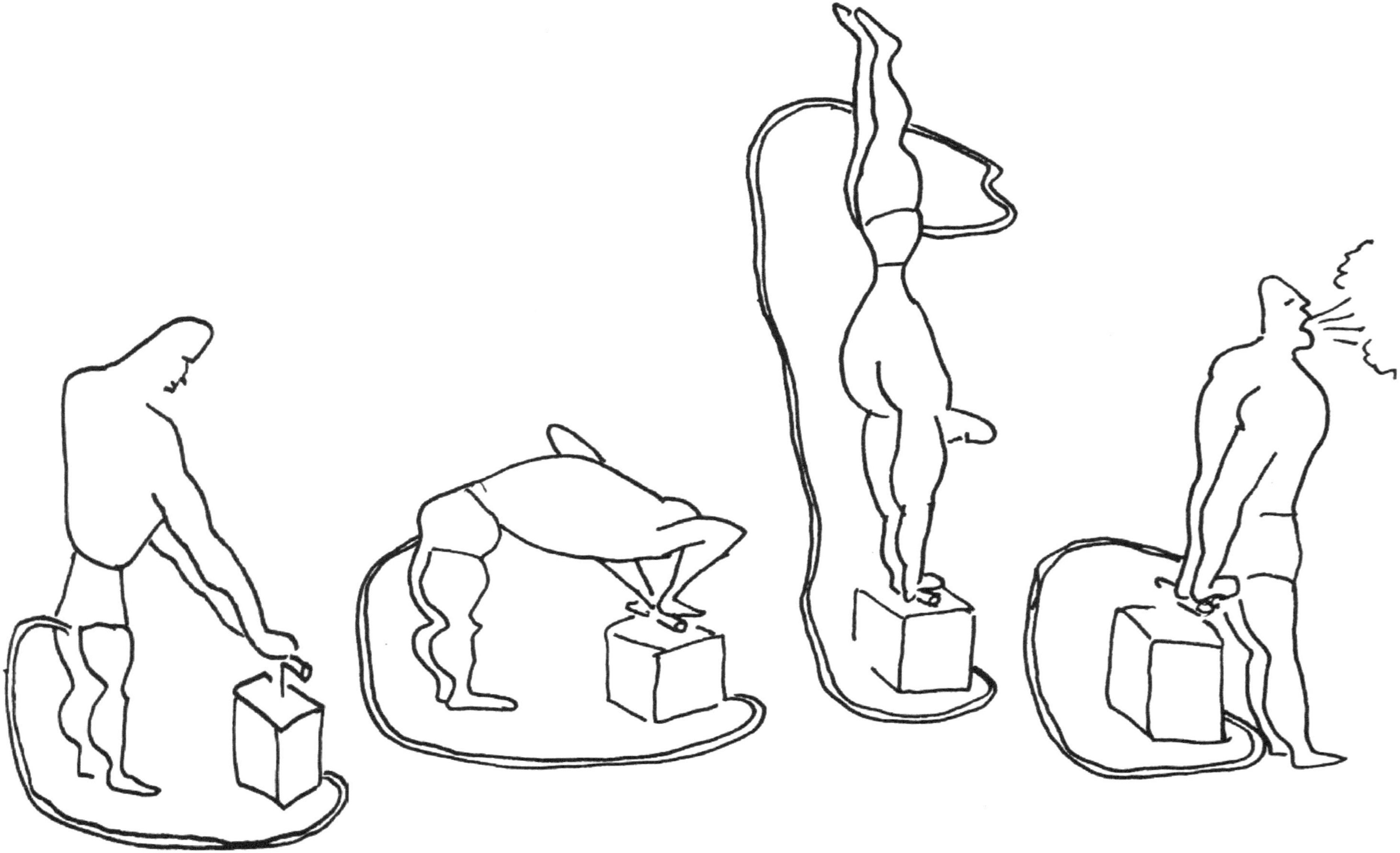

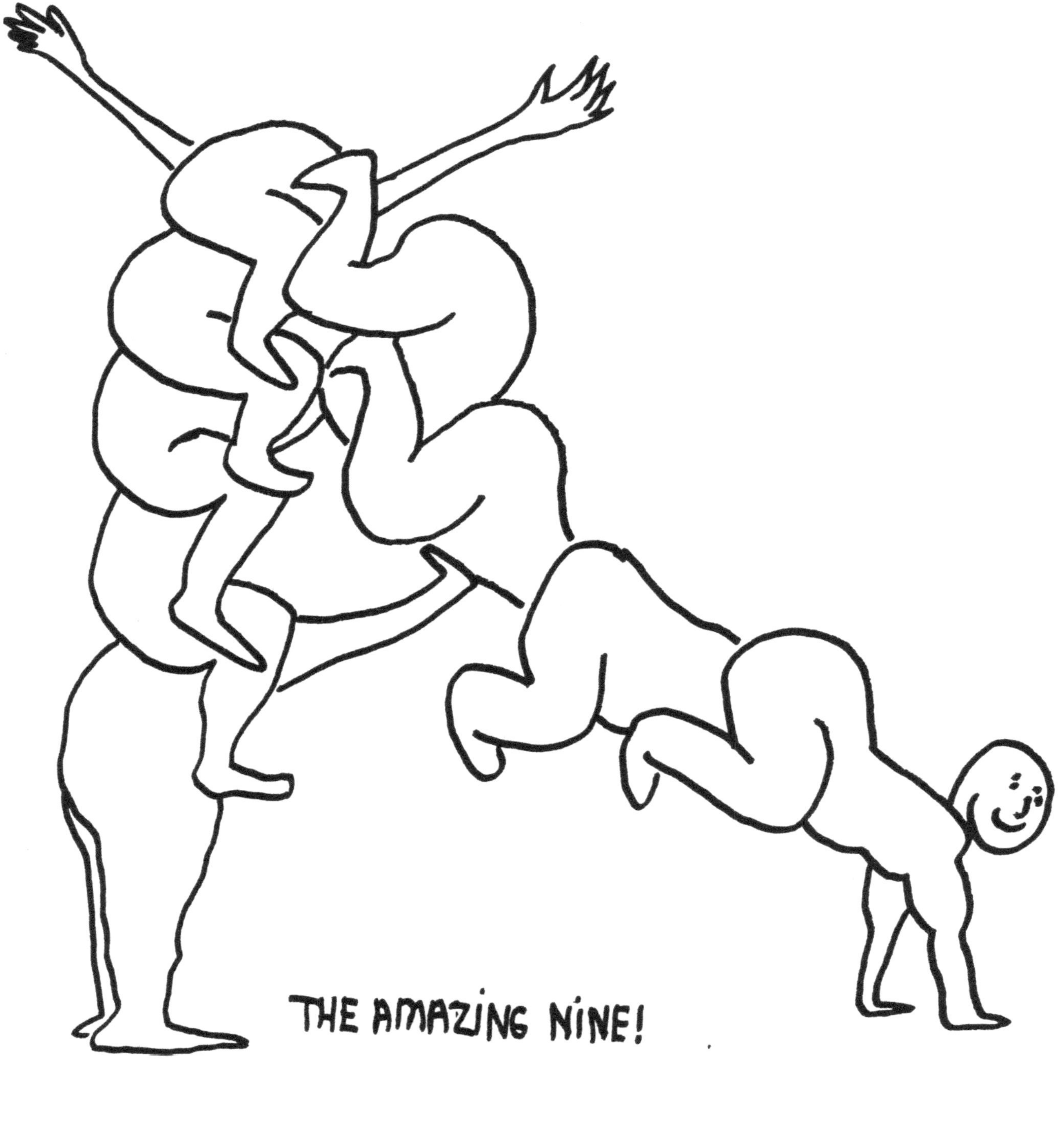
THE AMAZING NINE!

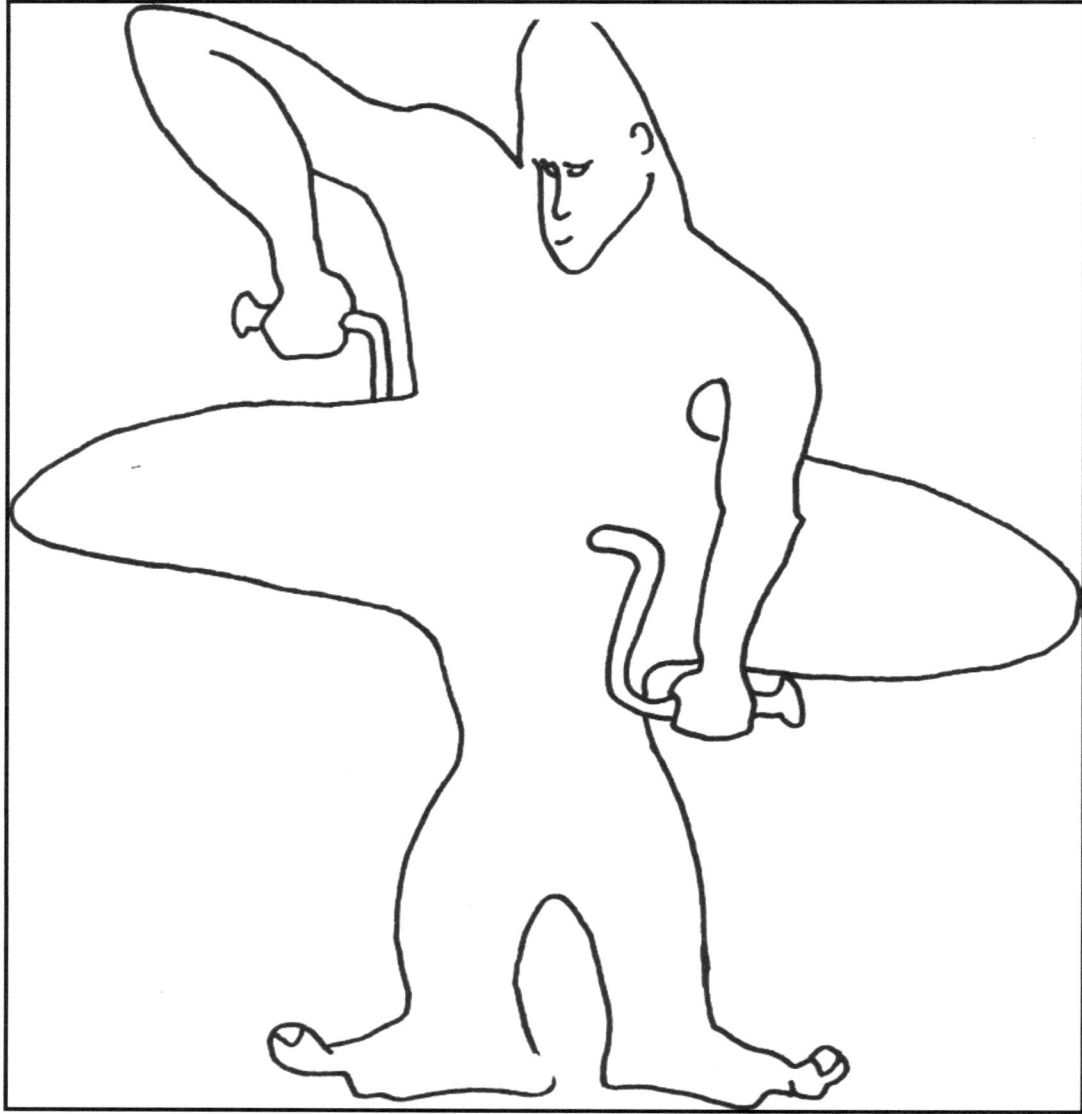

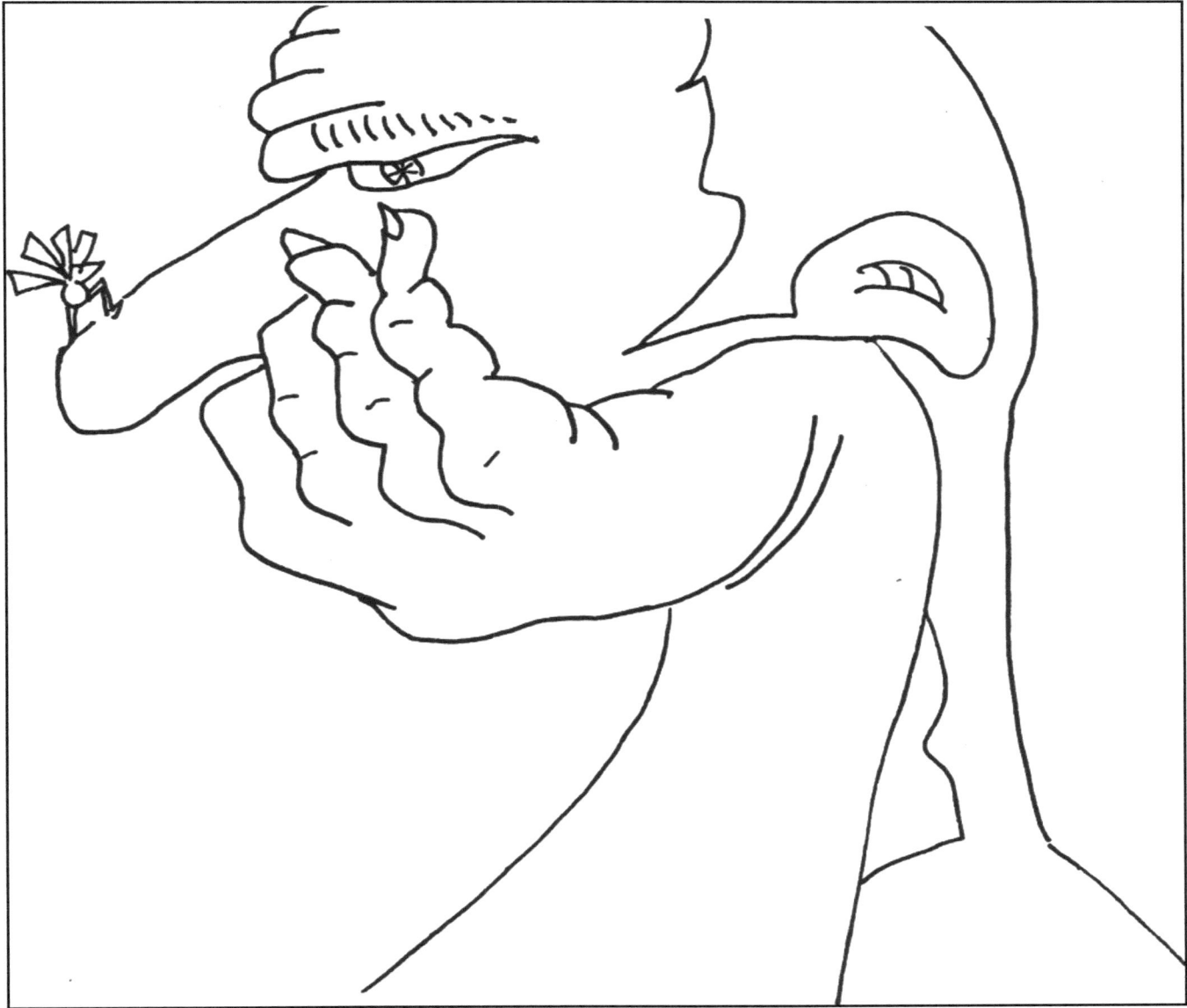

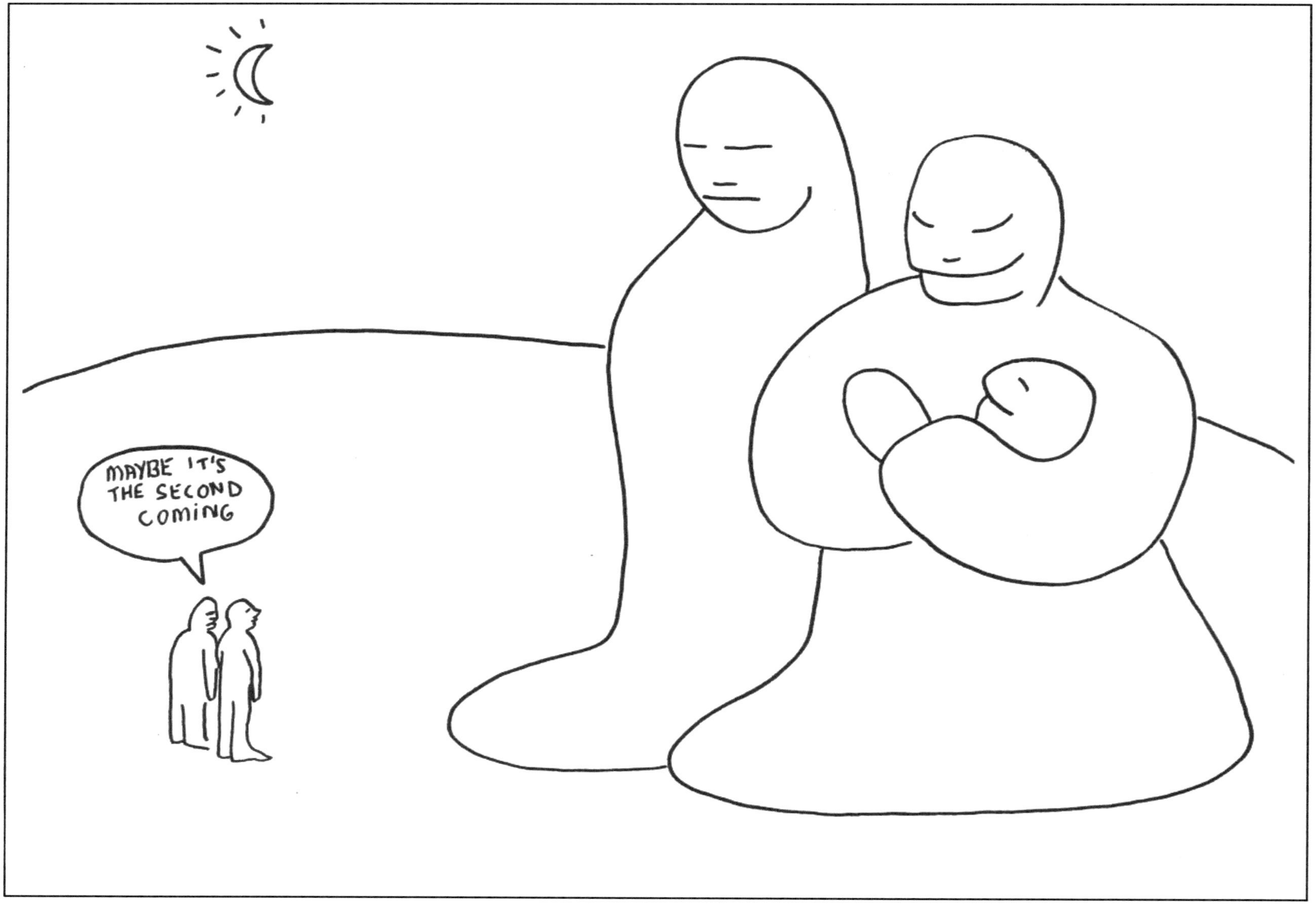
MAYBE IT'S THE SECOND COMING

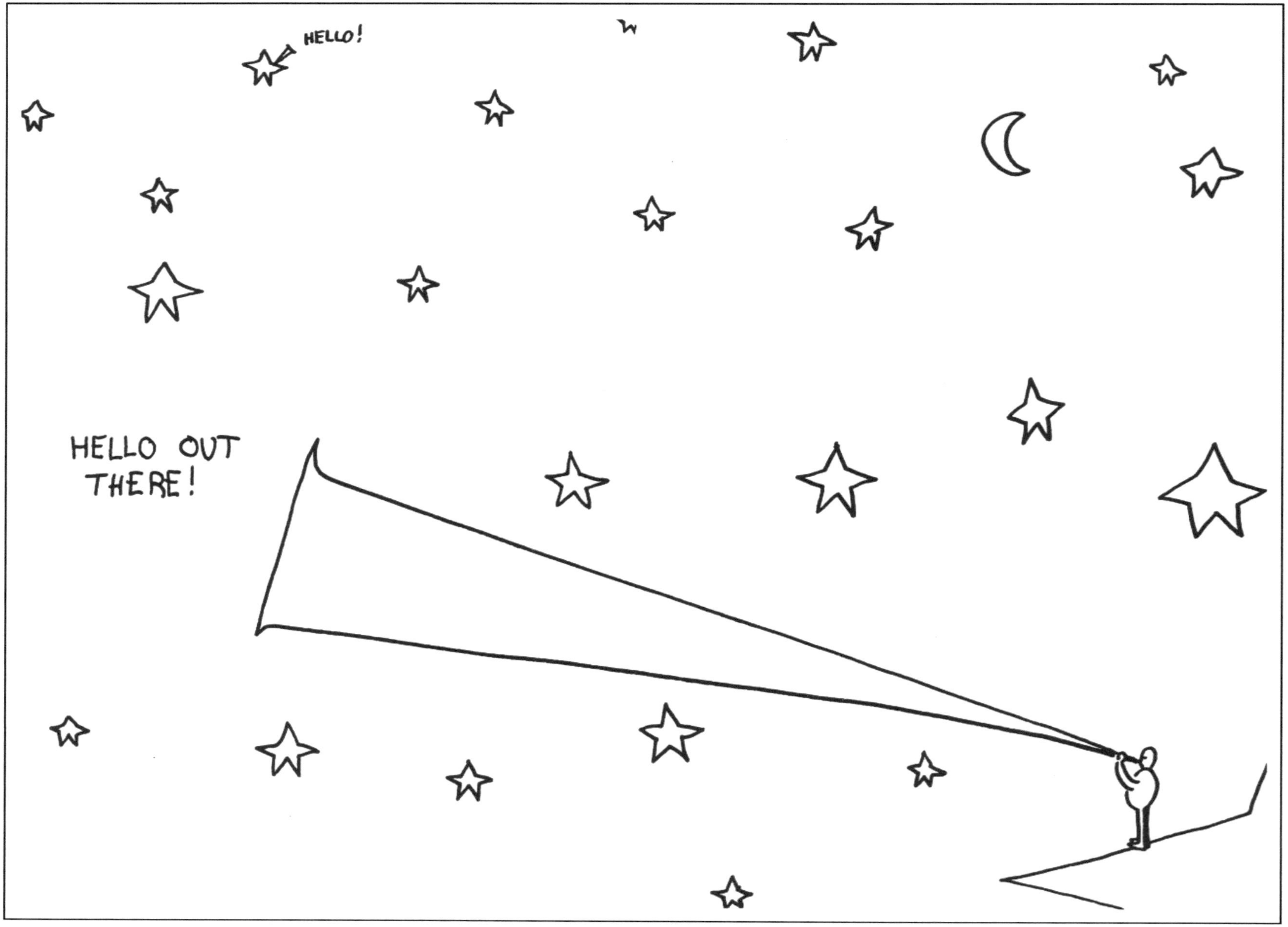
HELLO!
HELLO OUT THERE!

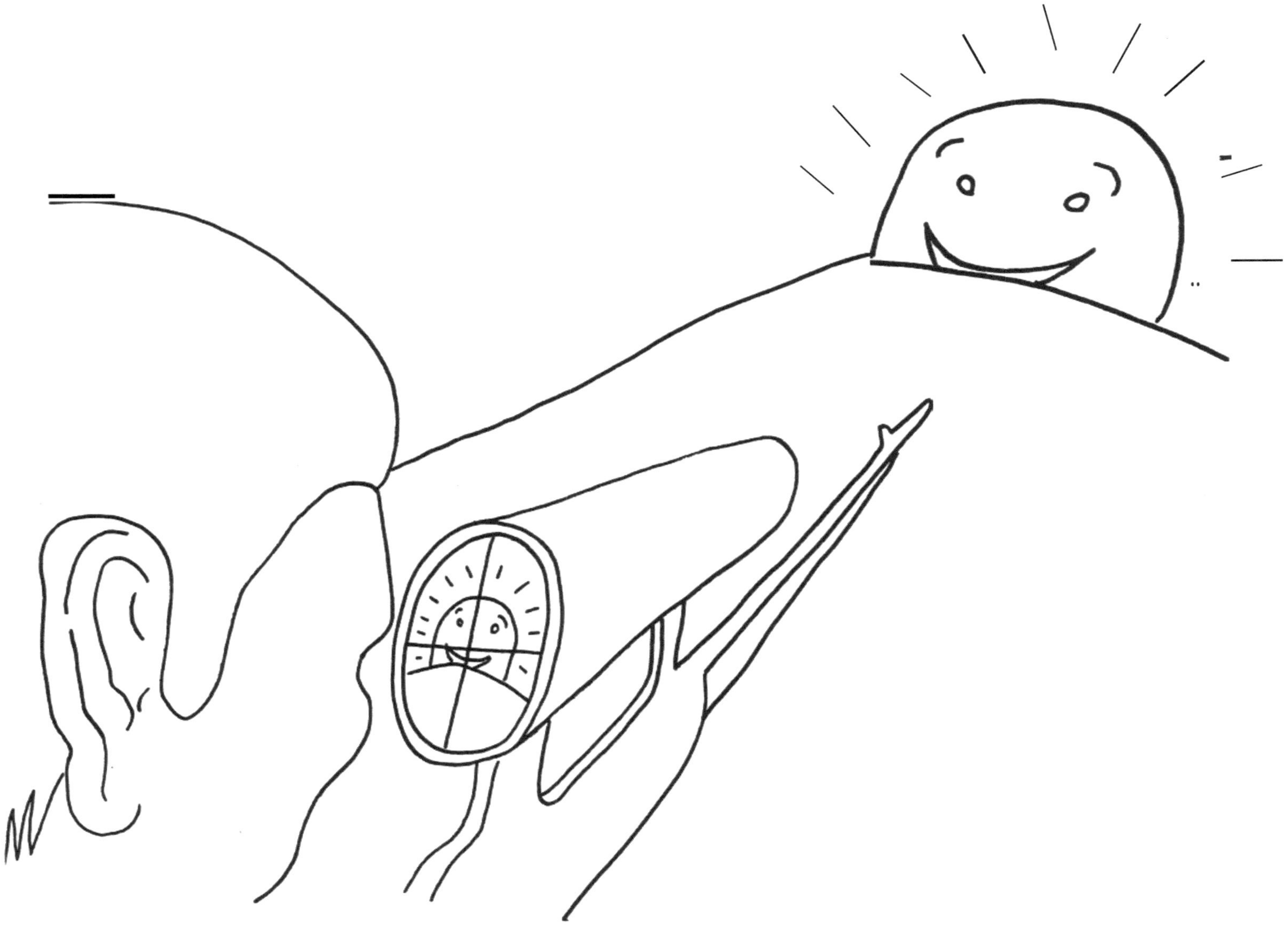

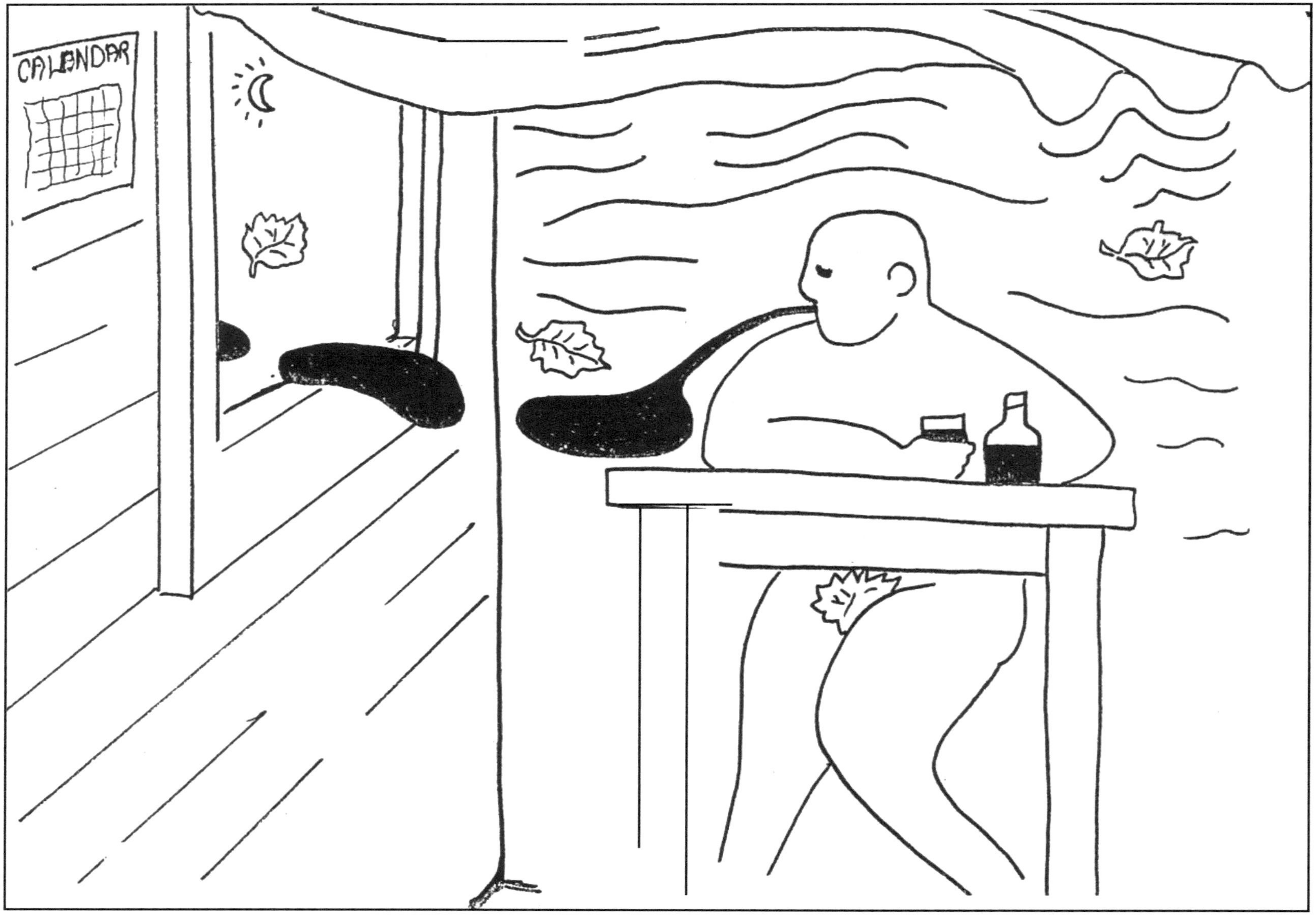
CALENDAR

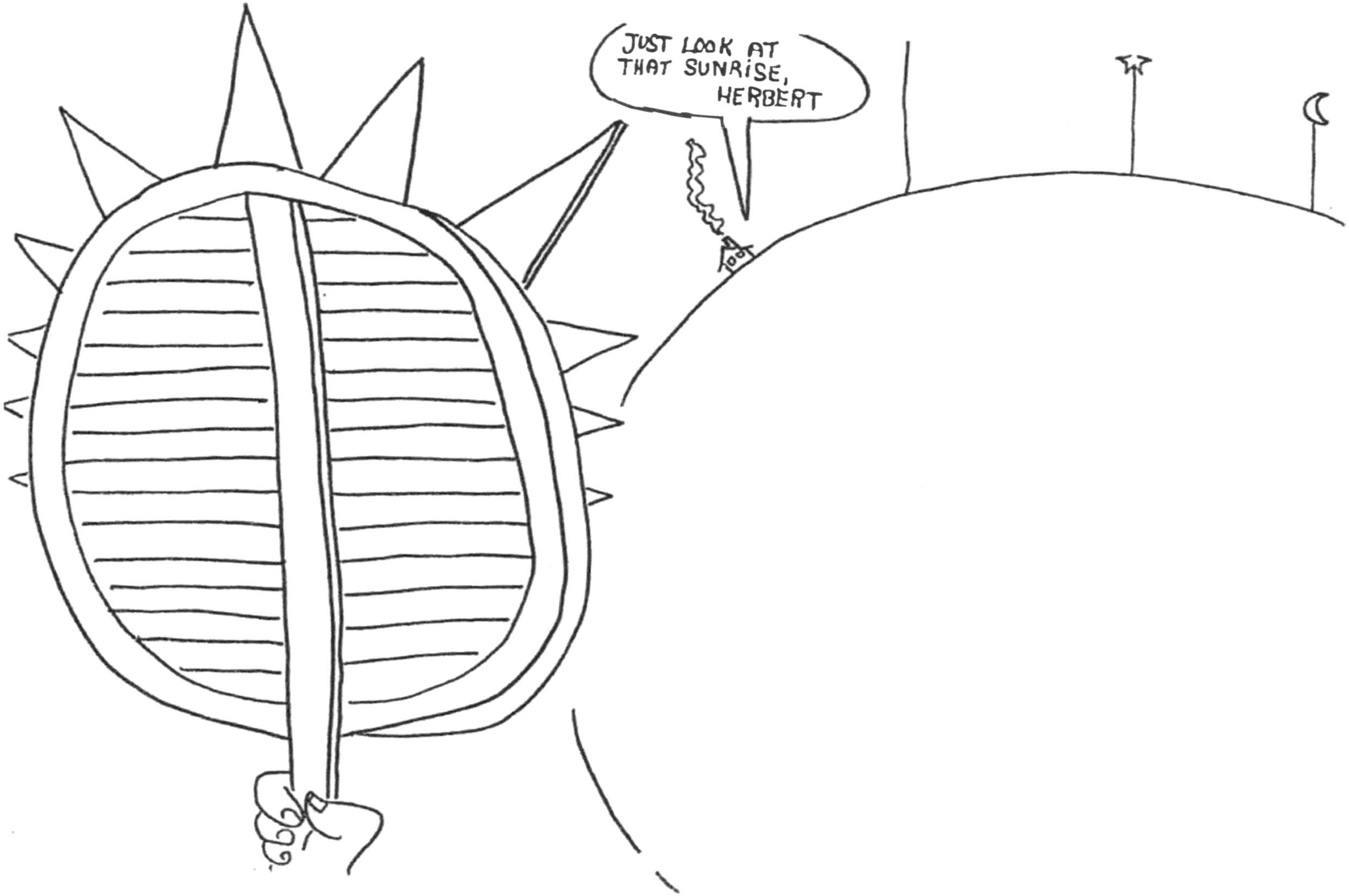
JUST LOOK AT THAT SUNRISE, HERBERT

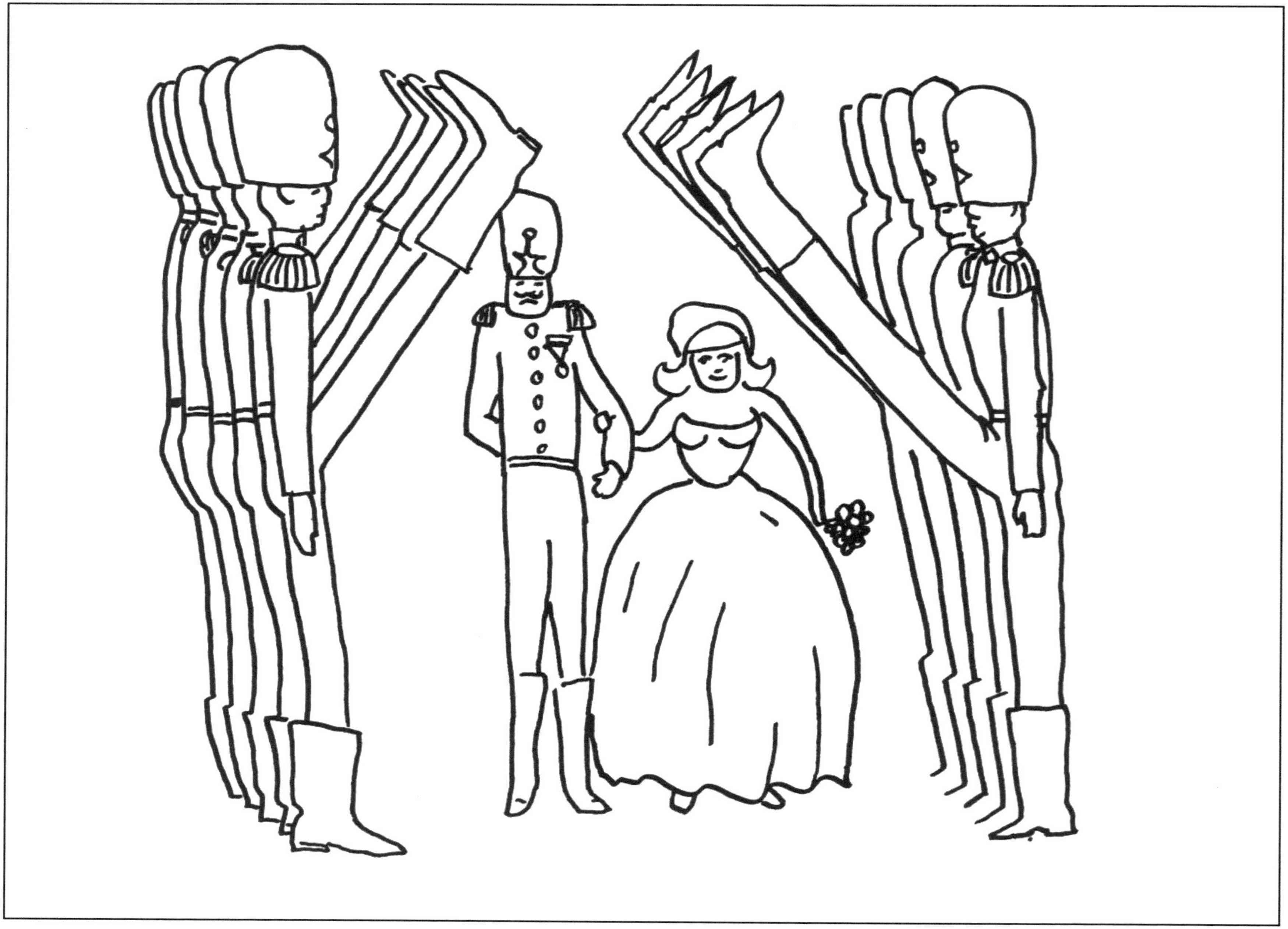

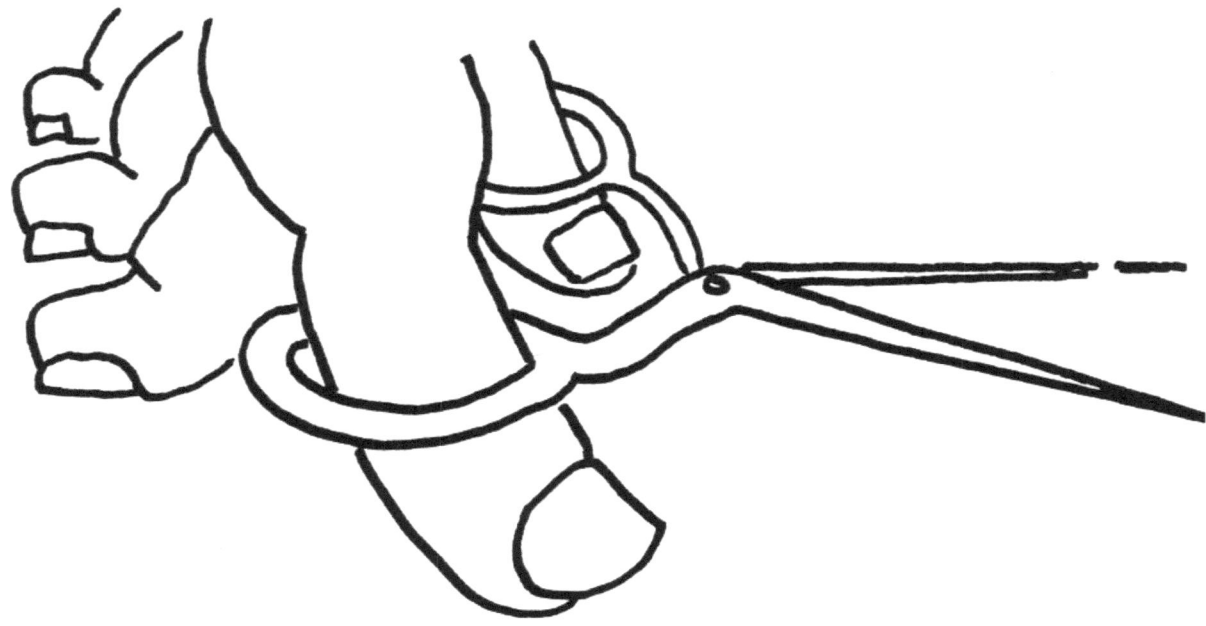

R.J.P.

STILL PISSED!

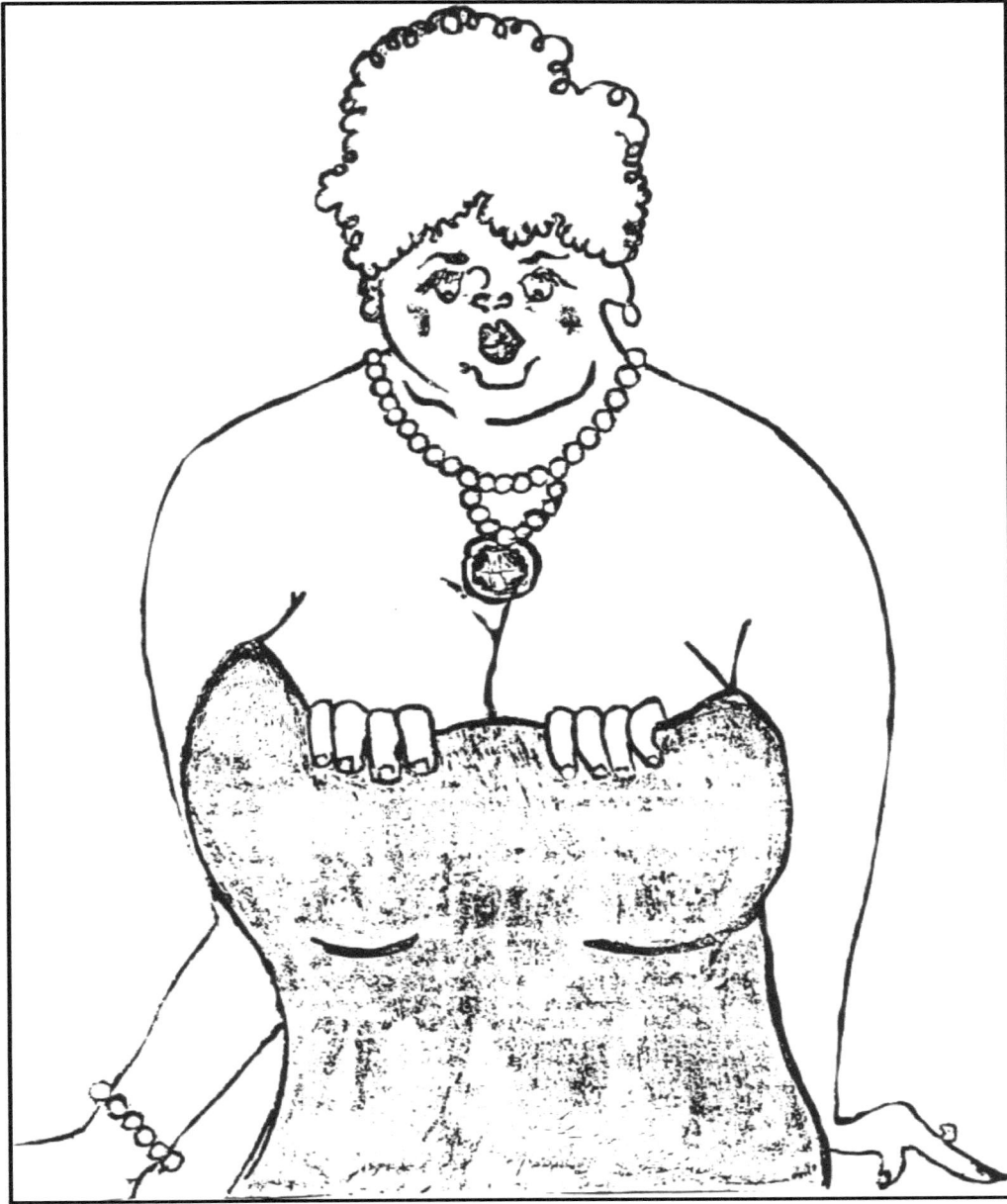

BIRDS, BEES AND FLOWERS

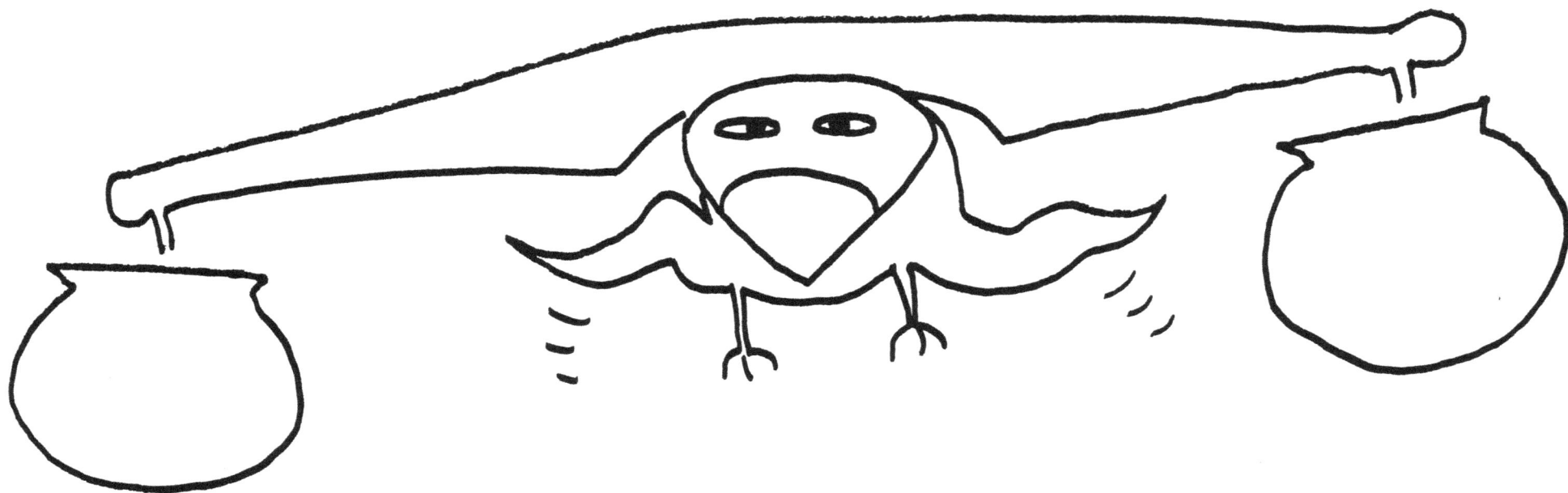

THE WITLESS WATERBIRD

UDDER BIRD

LONG-BILLED
STABBERS

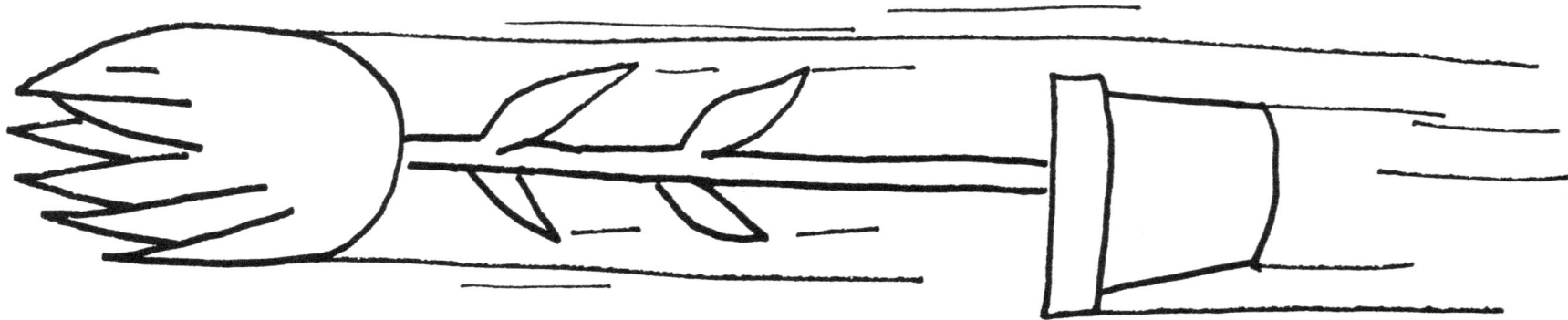

FLIGHT OF THE ROSE

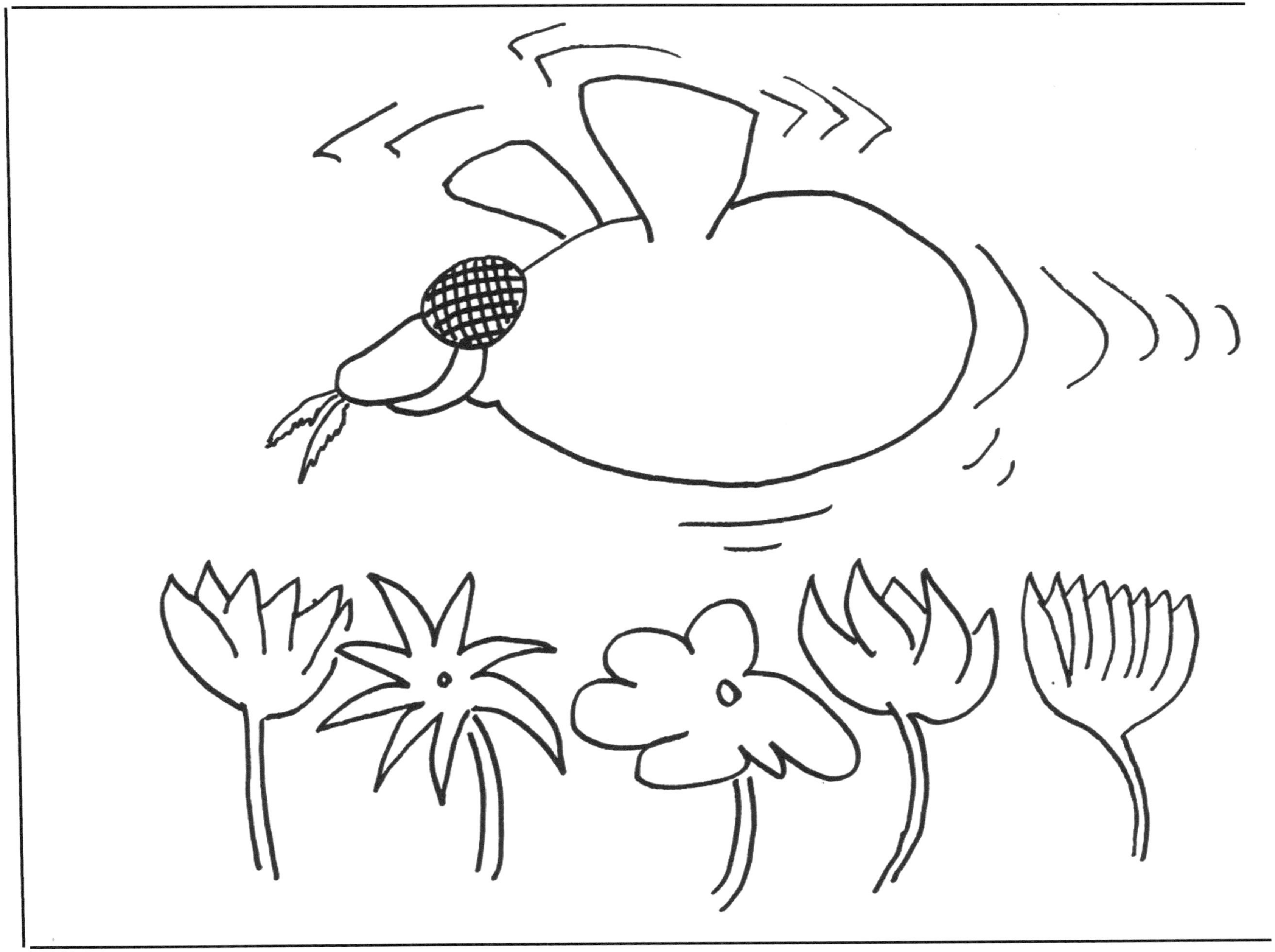

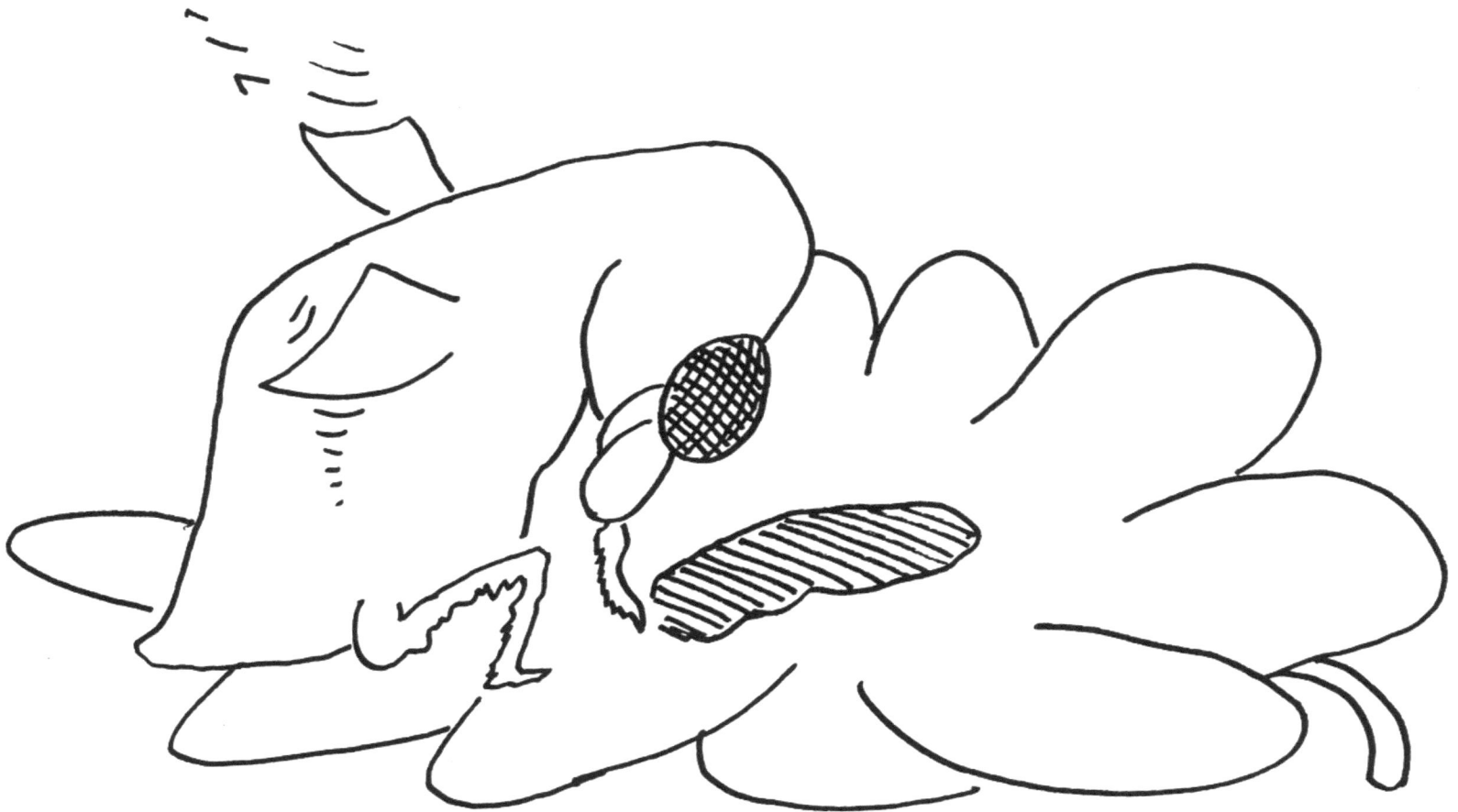

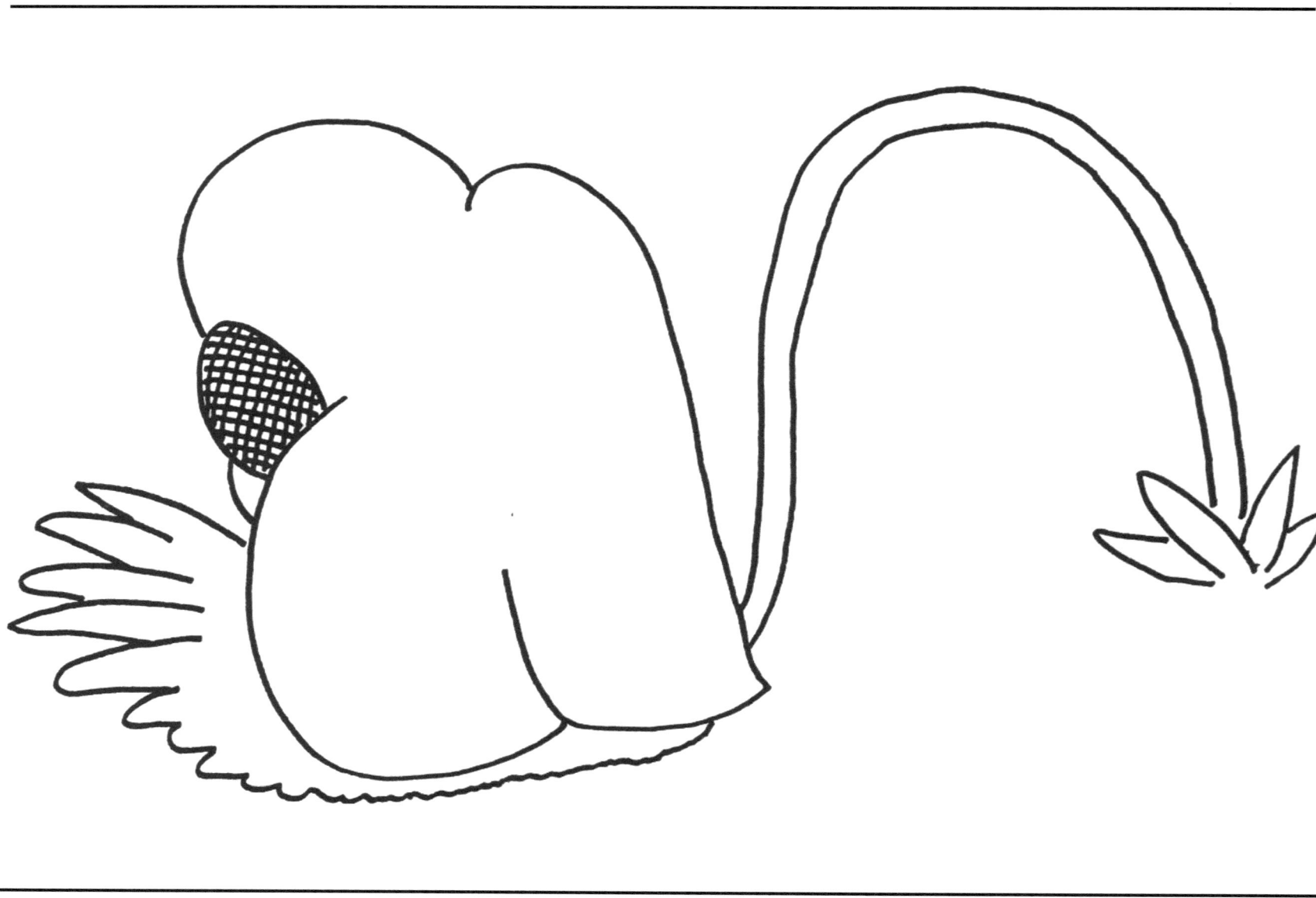

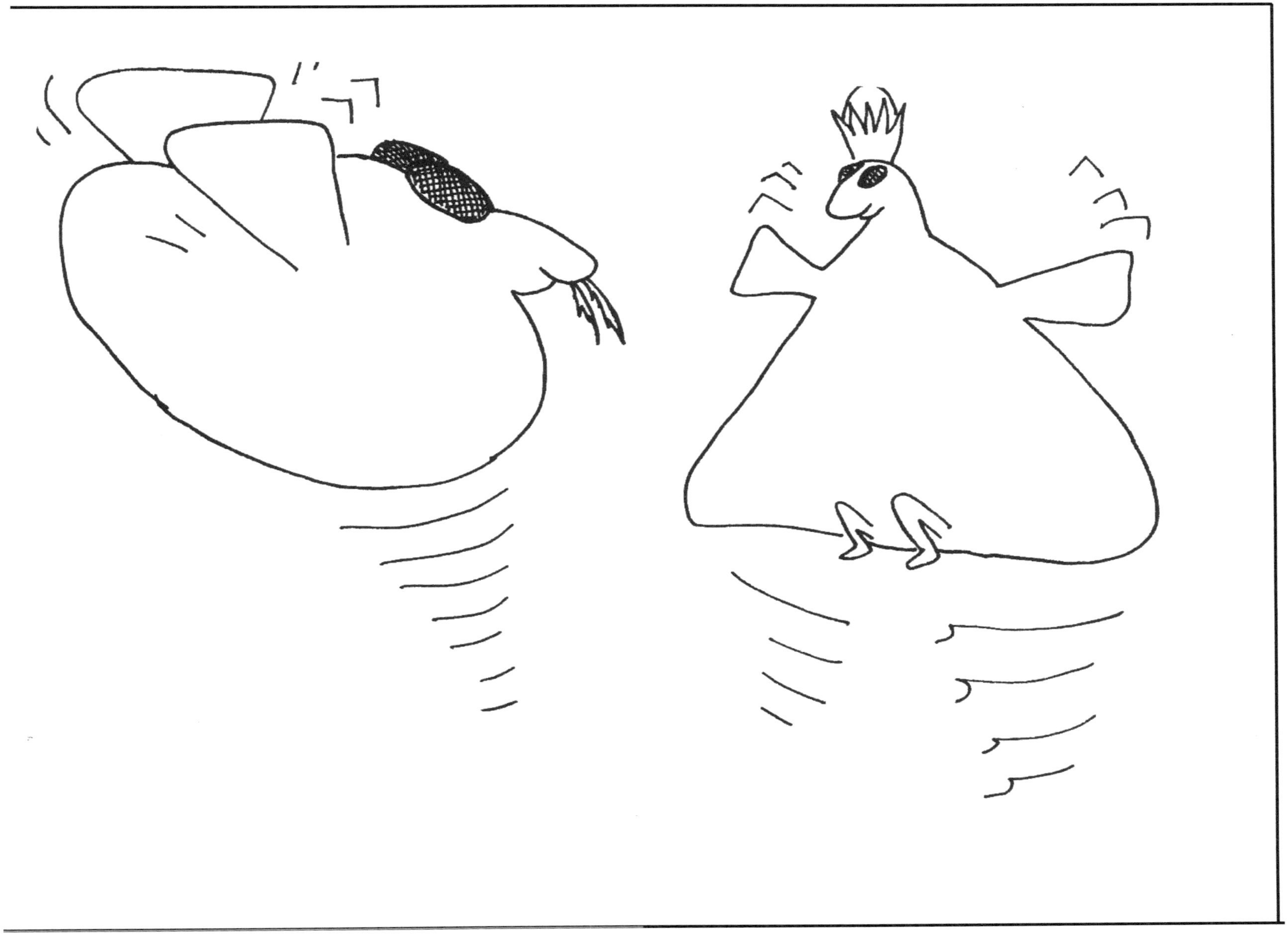

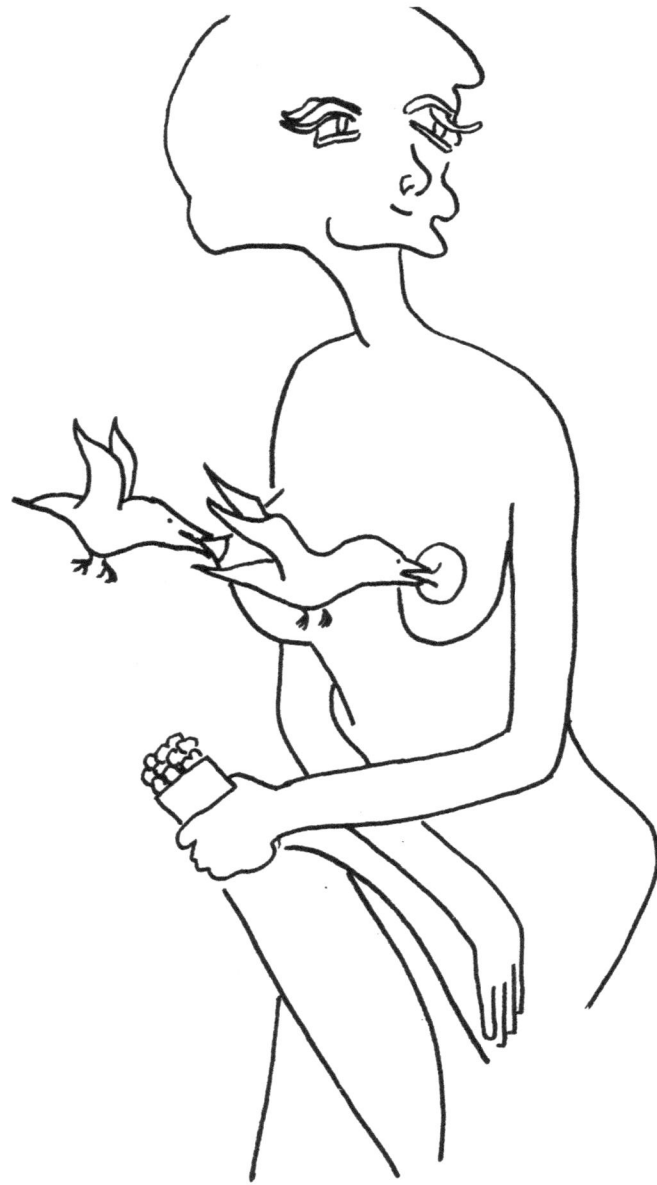

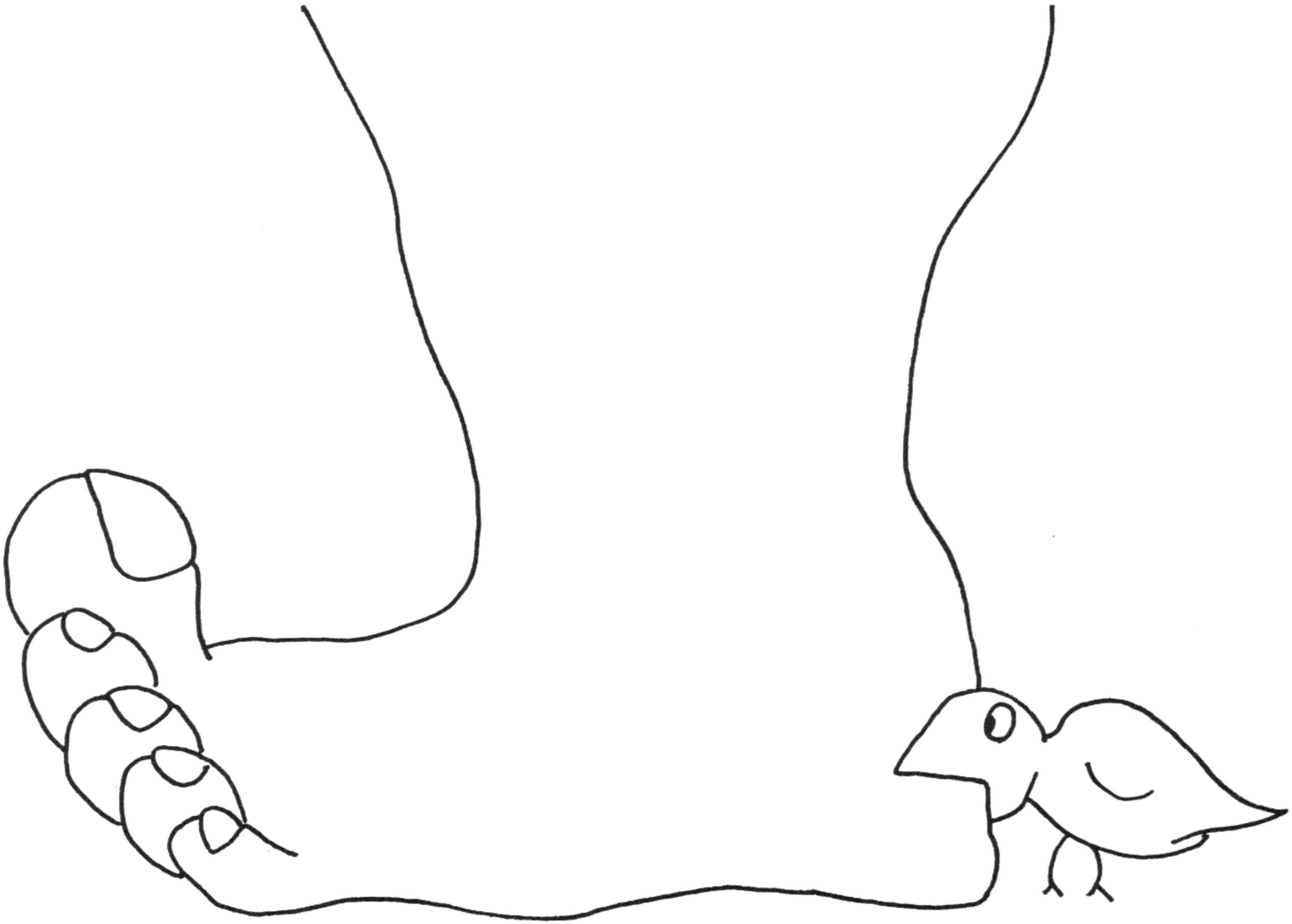

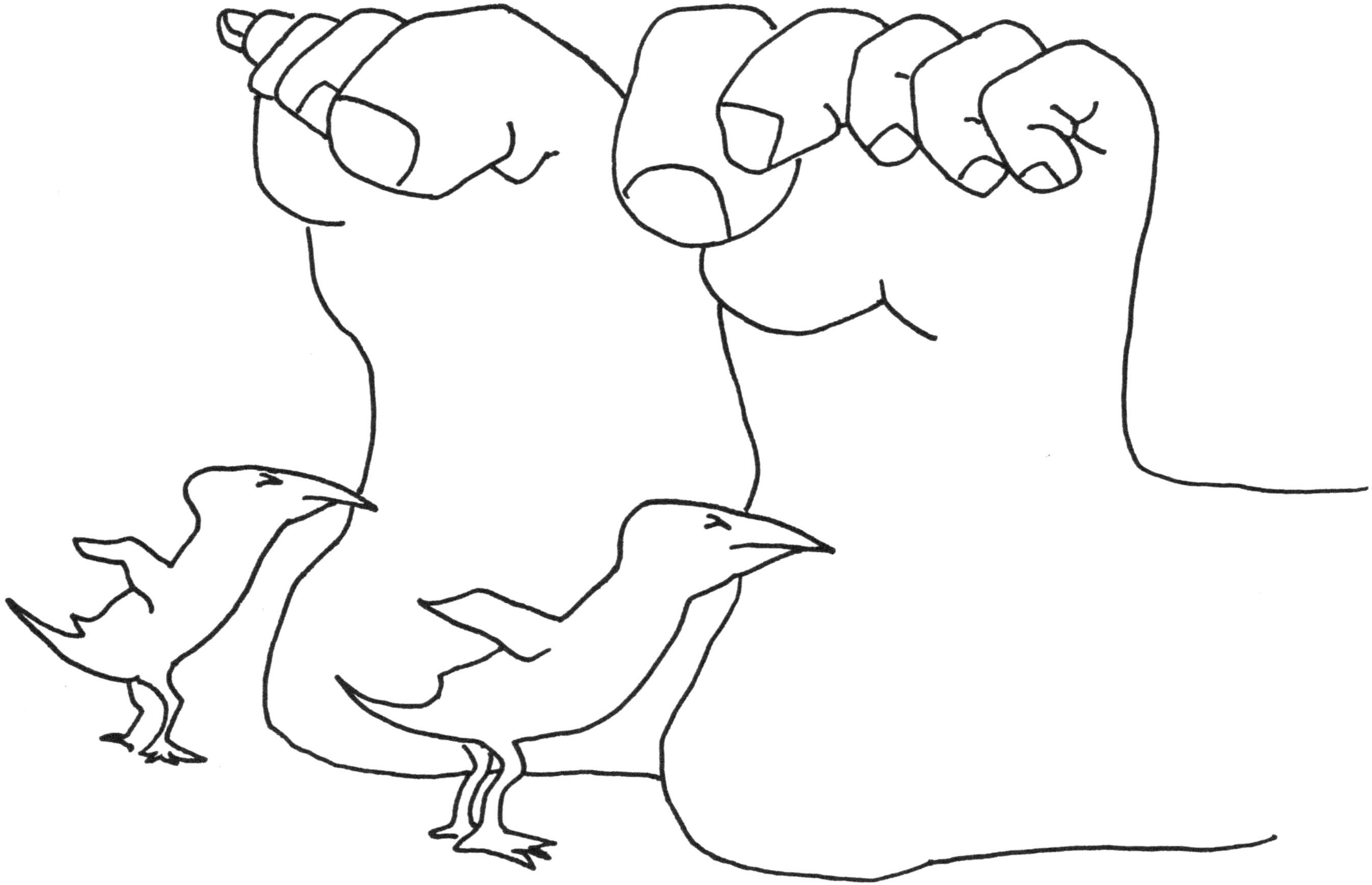

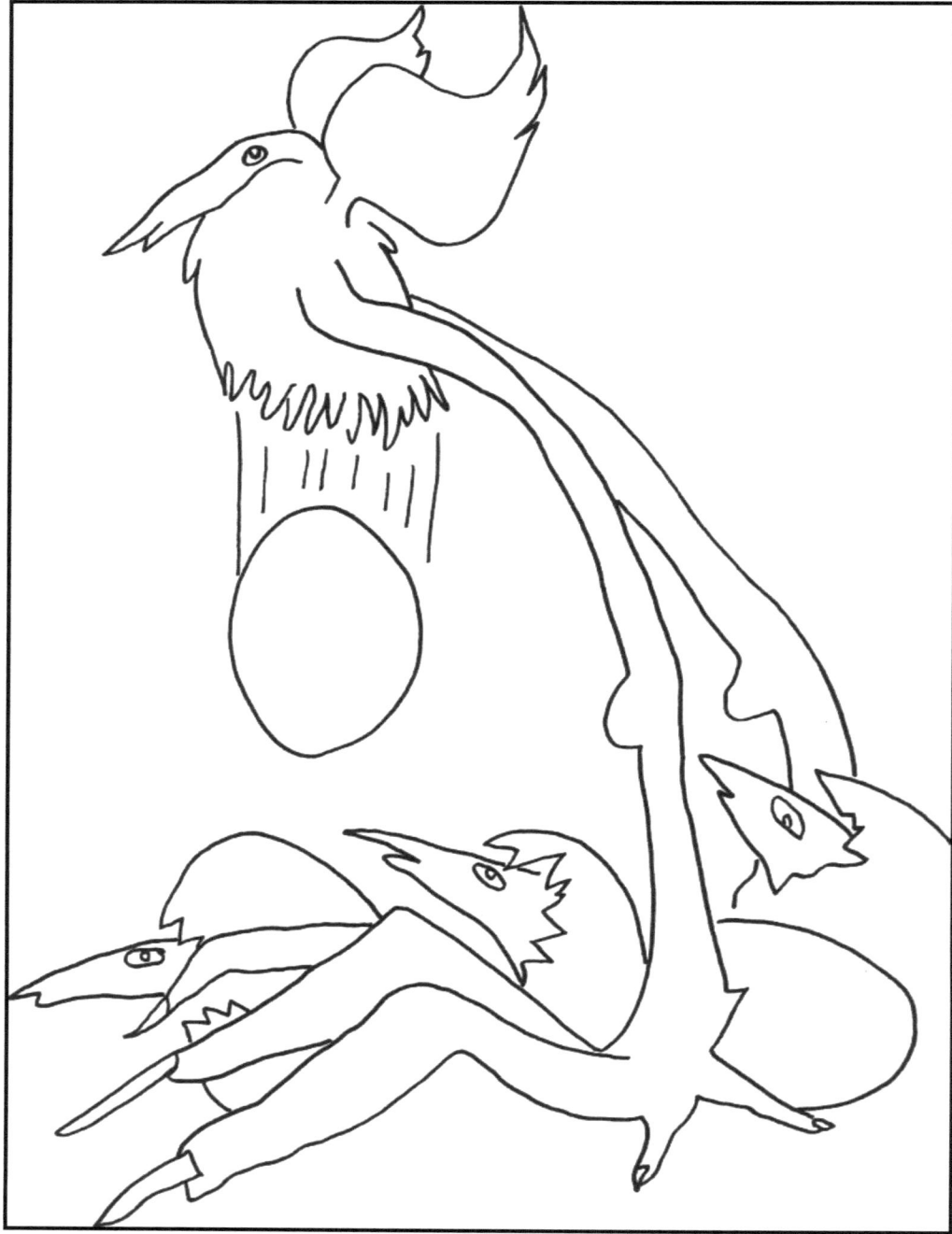

BIRDS OF A FEATHER

CREATURES

MOON FOR THE MISBEGOTTEN?

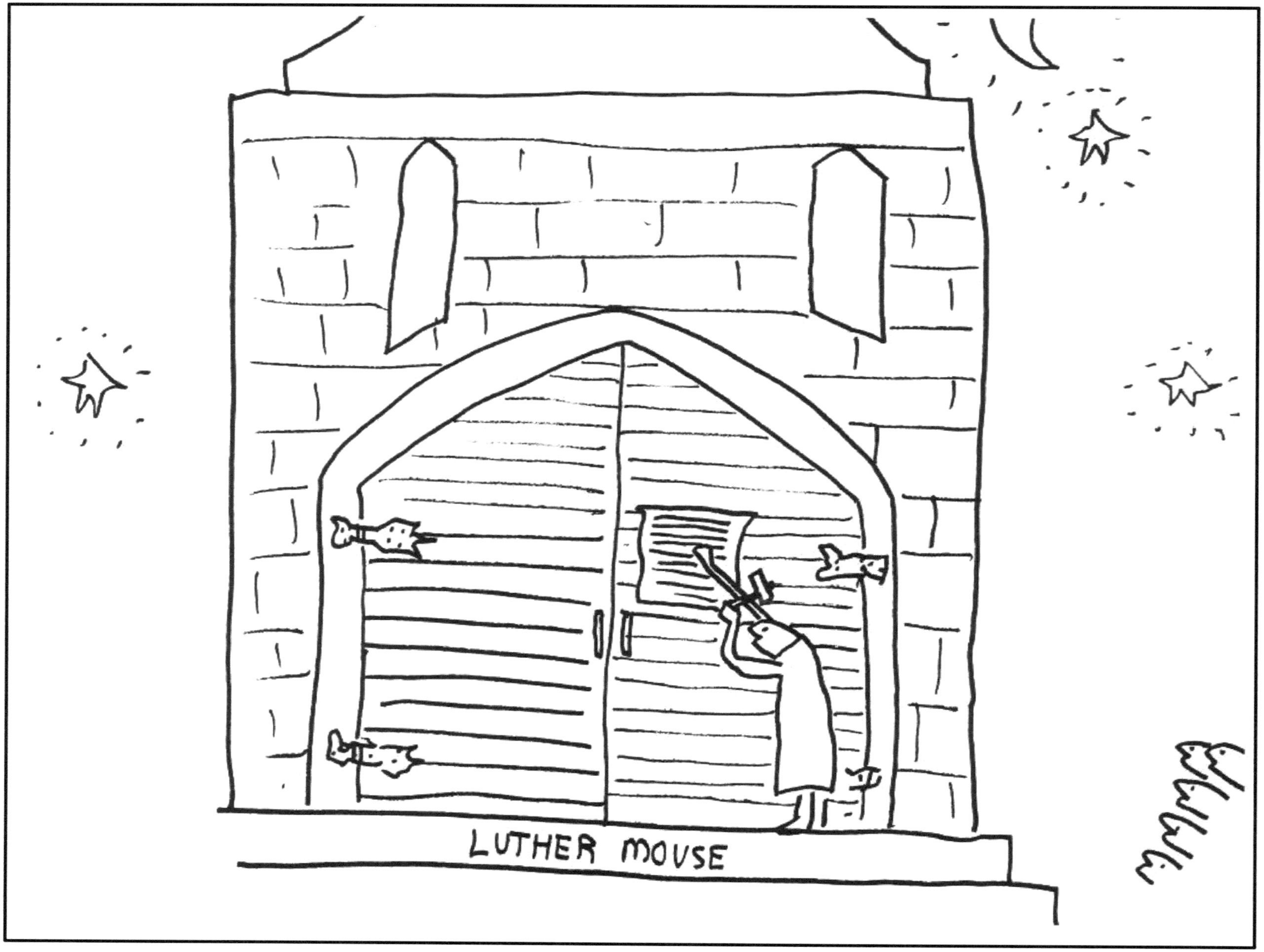
LUTHER MOUSE

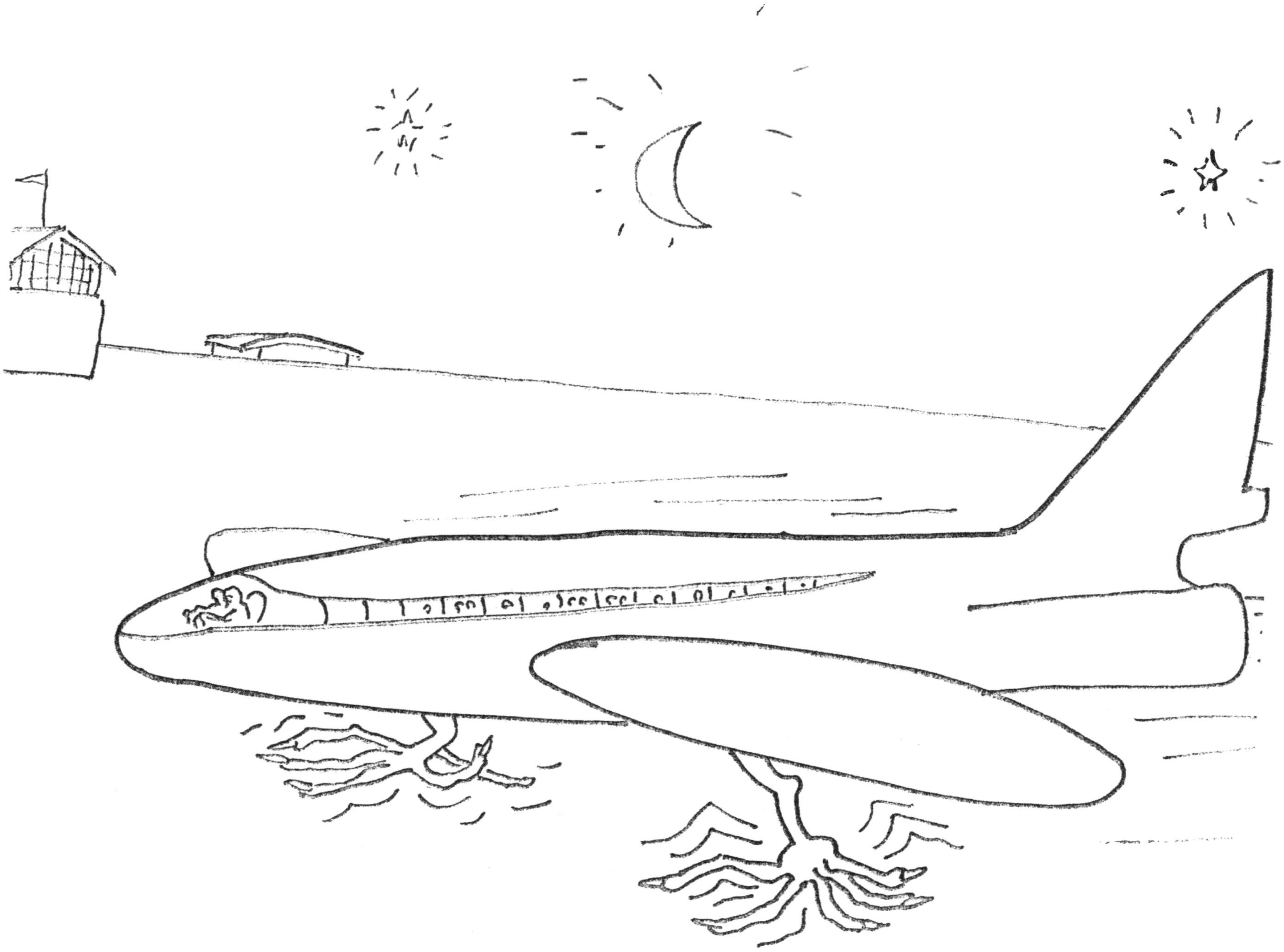

THREE-FLAVORS MOUSE

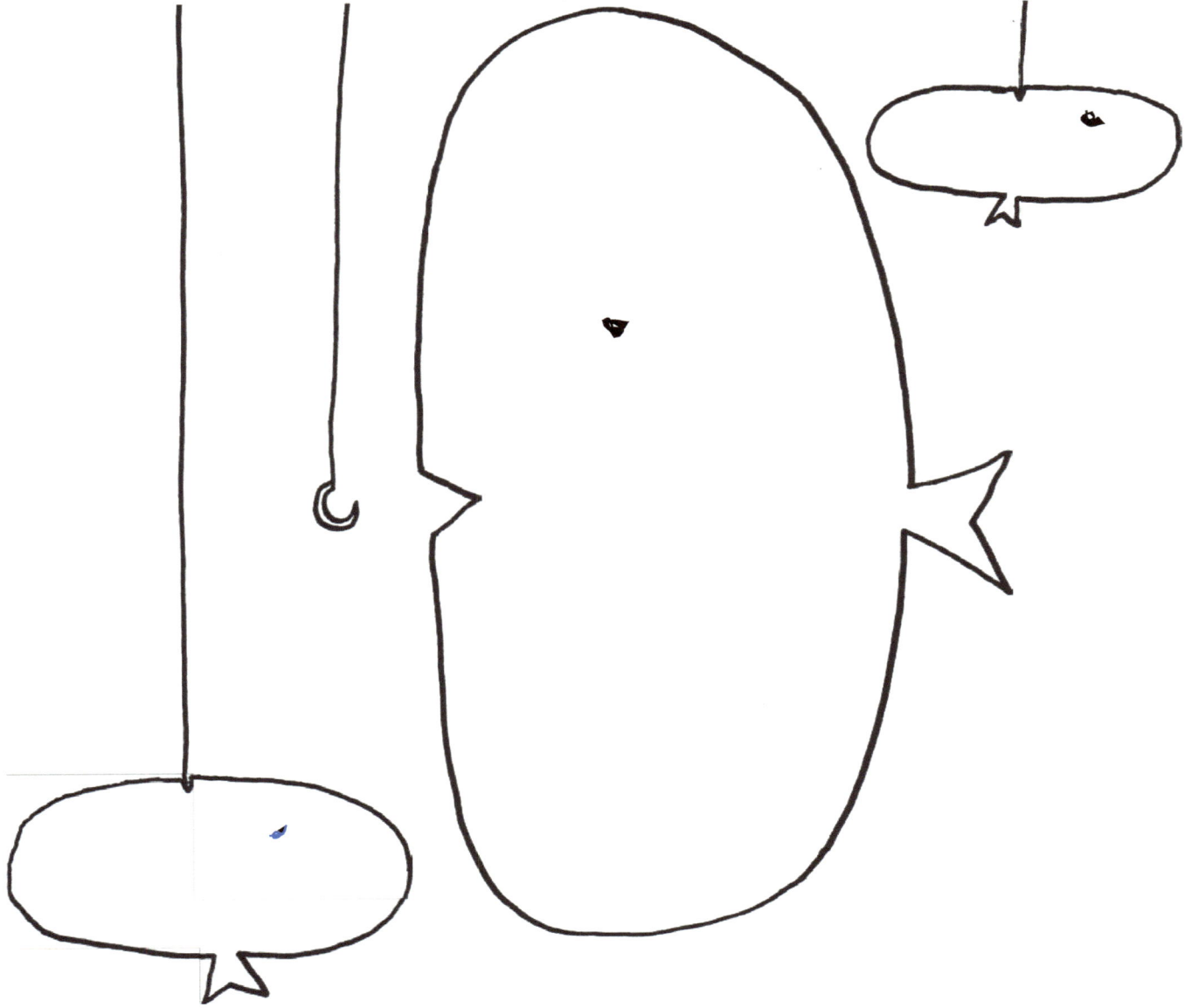

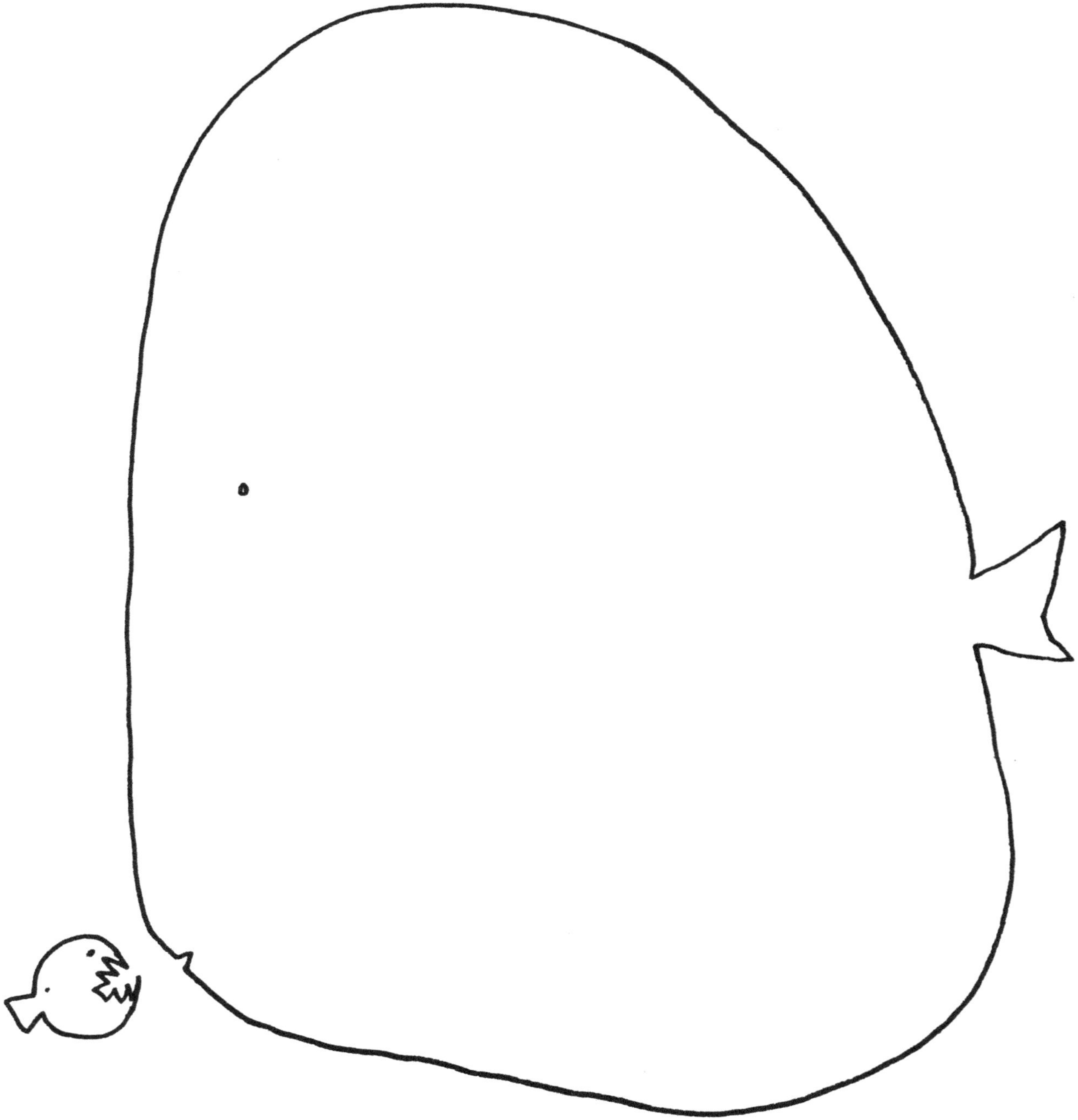

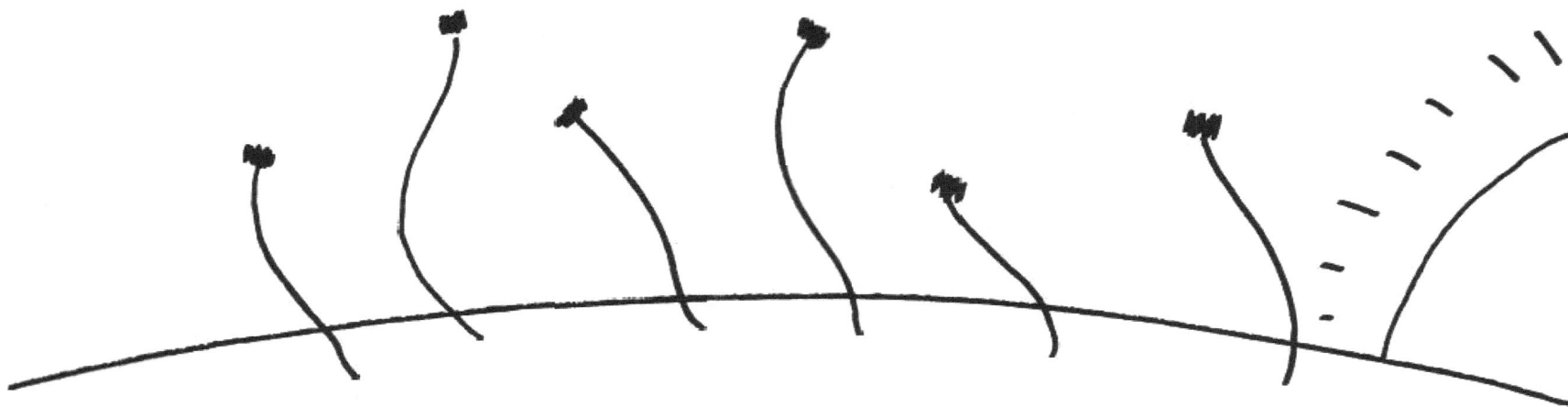

A FIELD OF HITLER'S-MUSTACHE

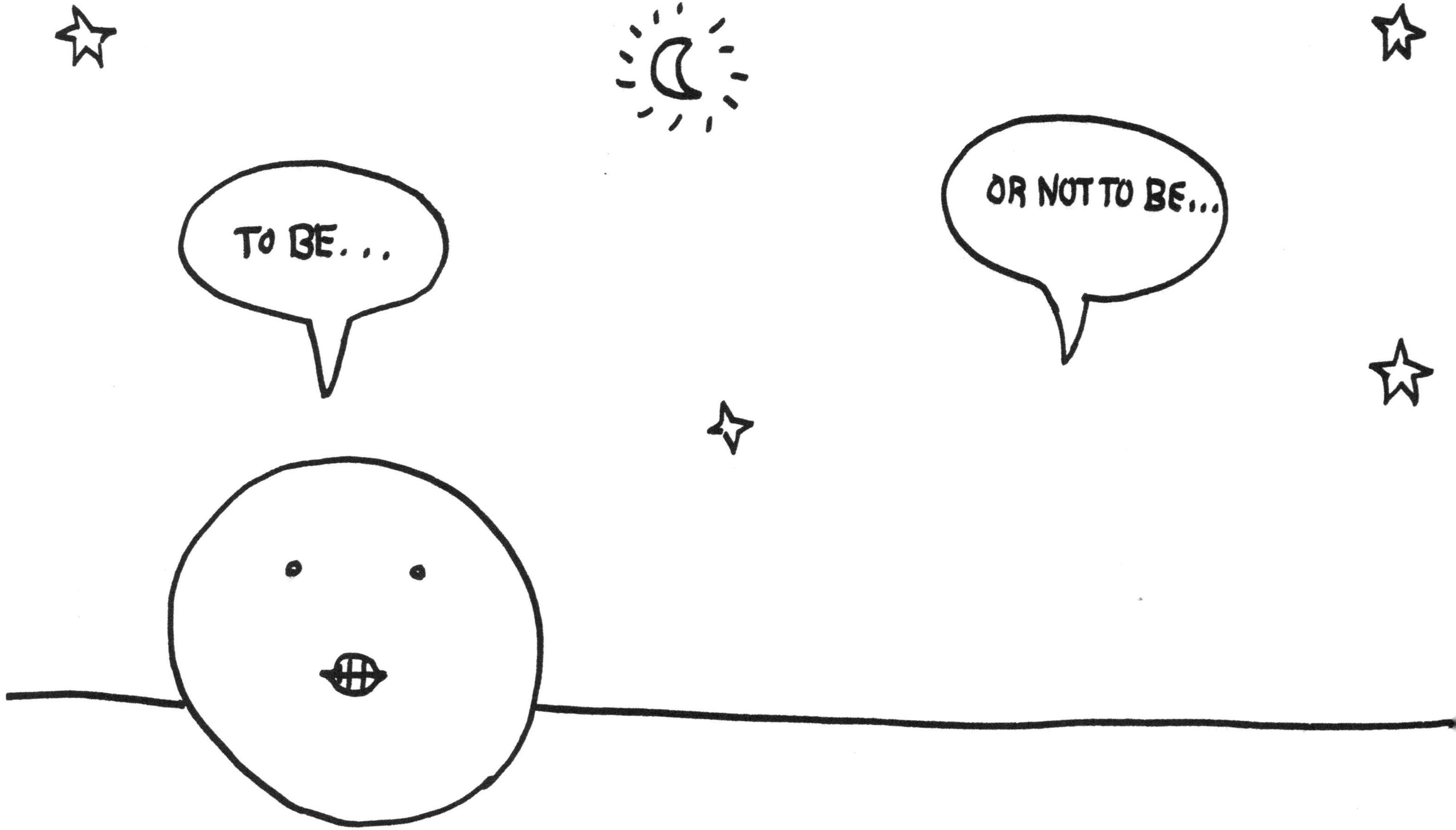
TO BE...
OR NOT TO BE...

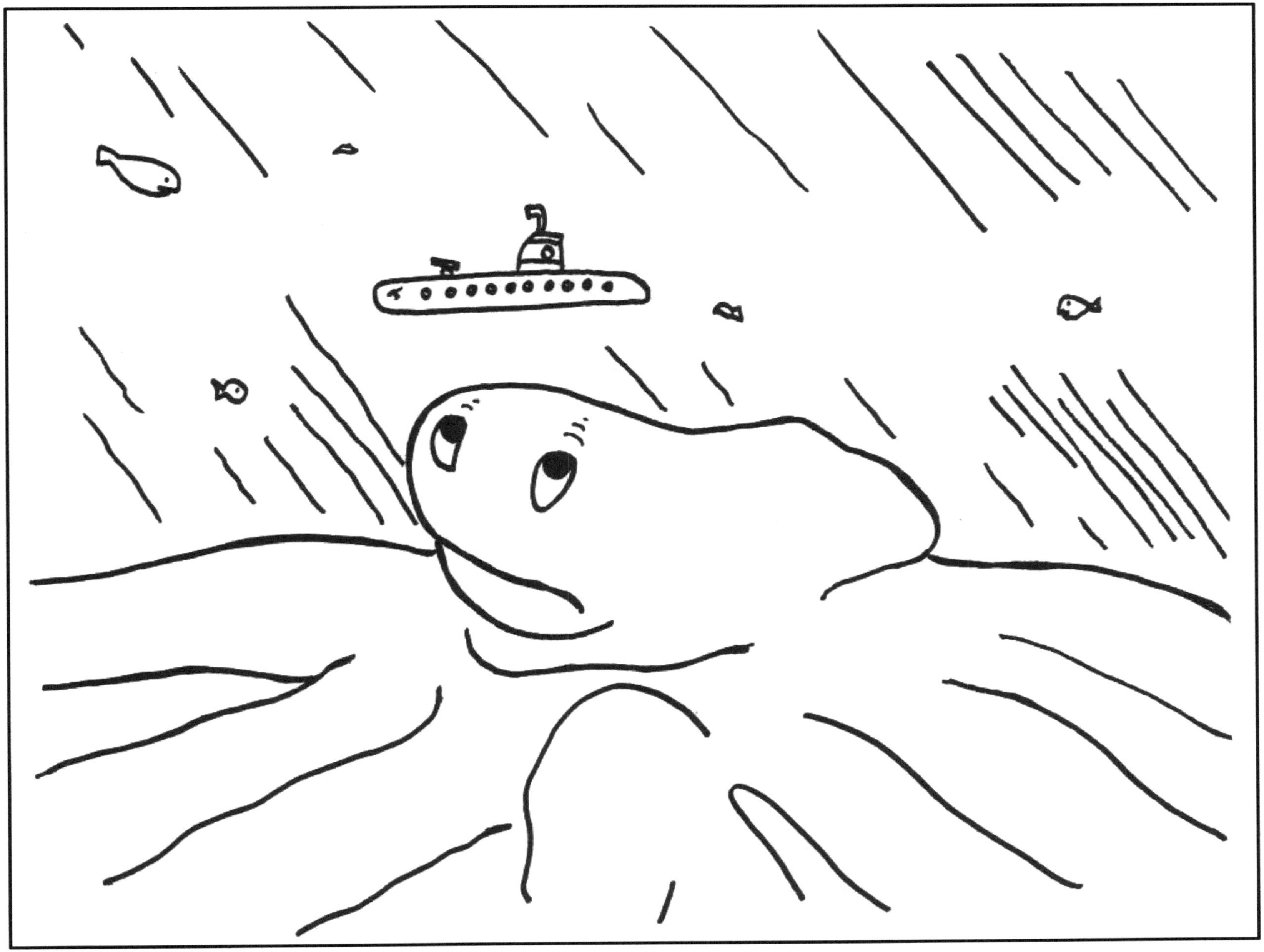

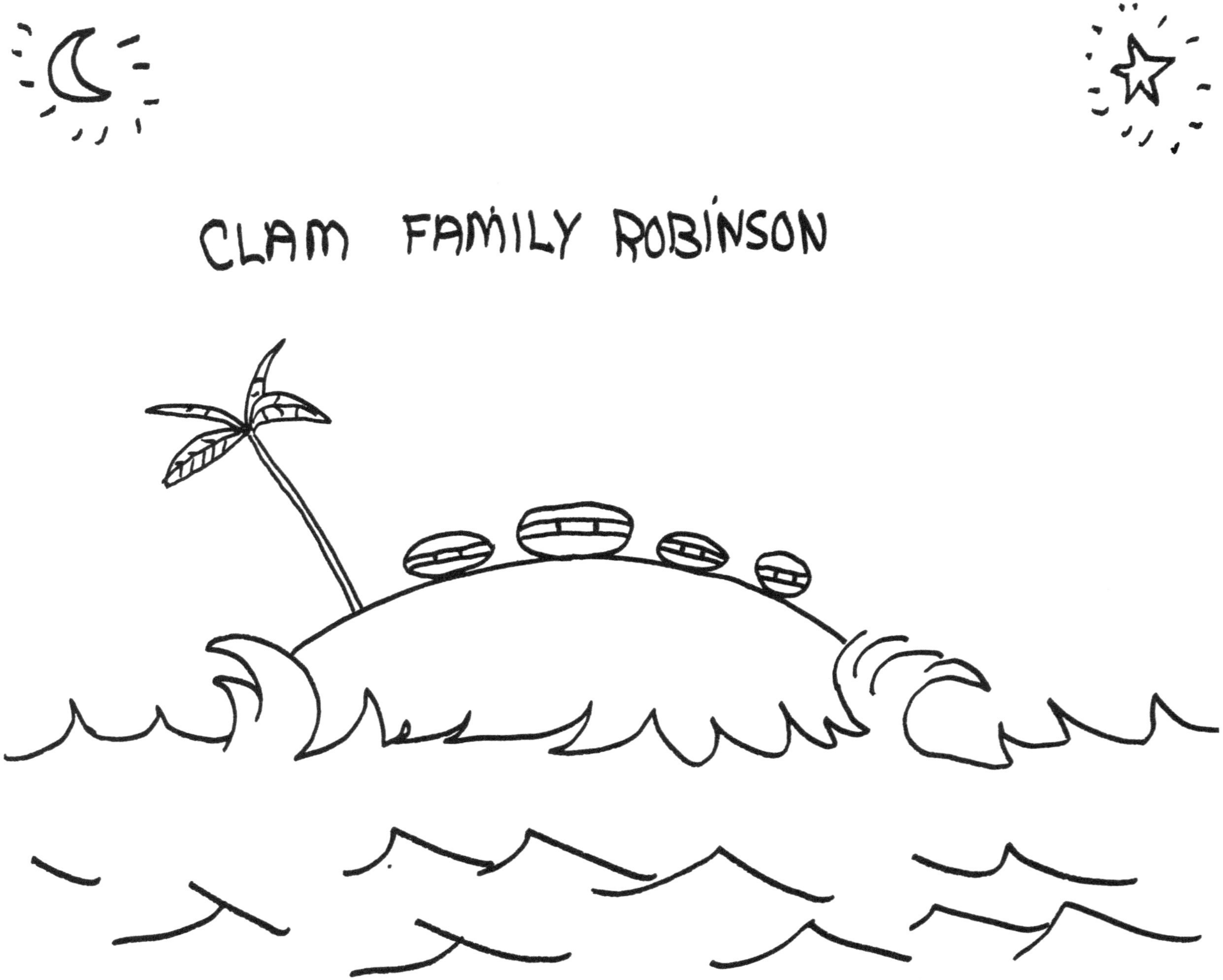
CLAM FAMILY ROBINSON

MISSING LINK

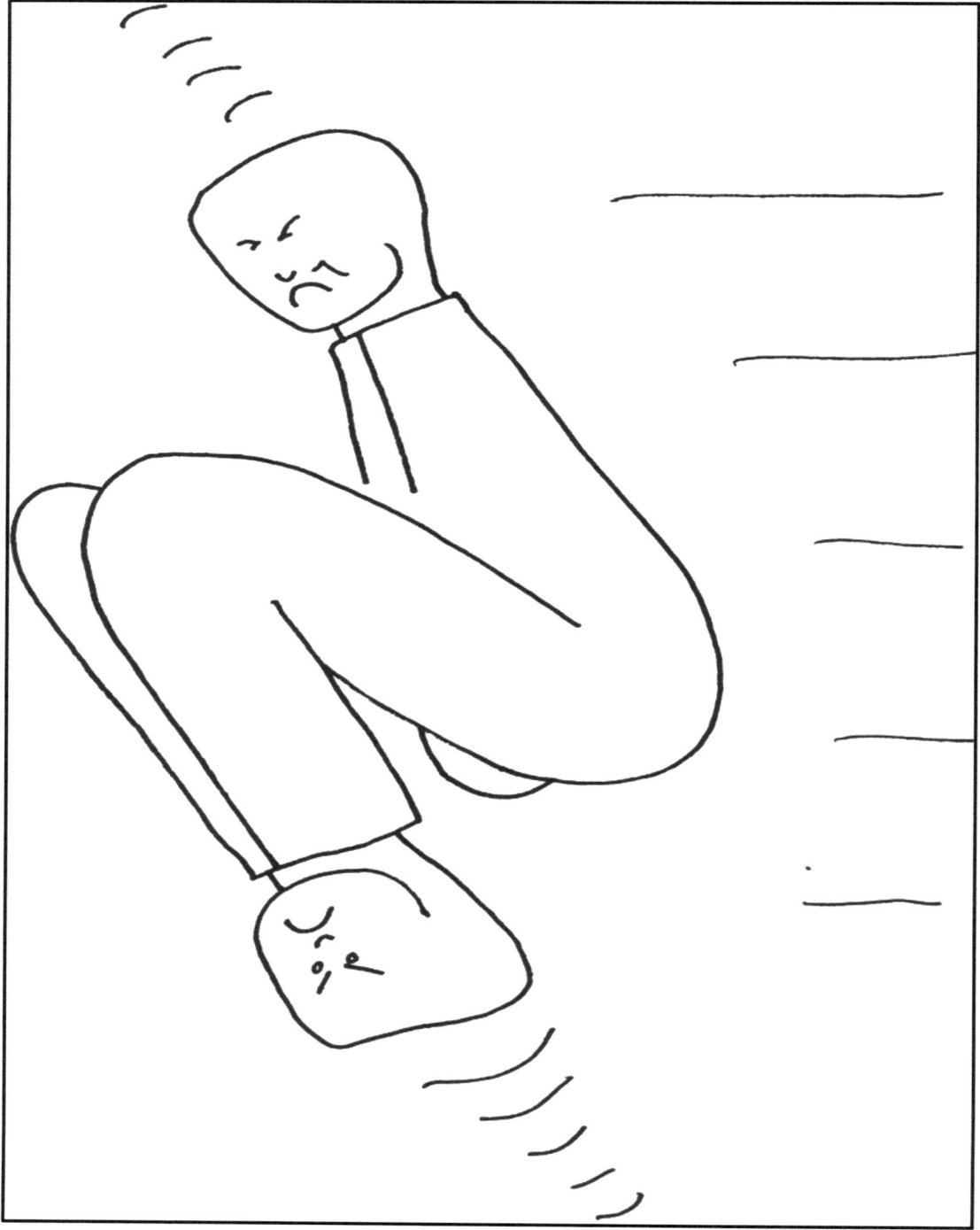

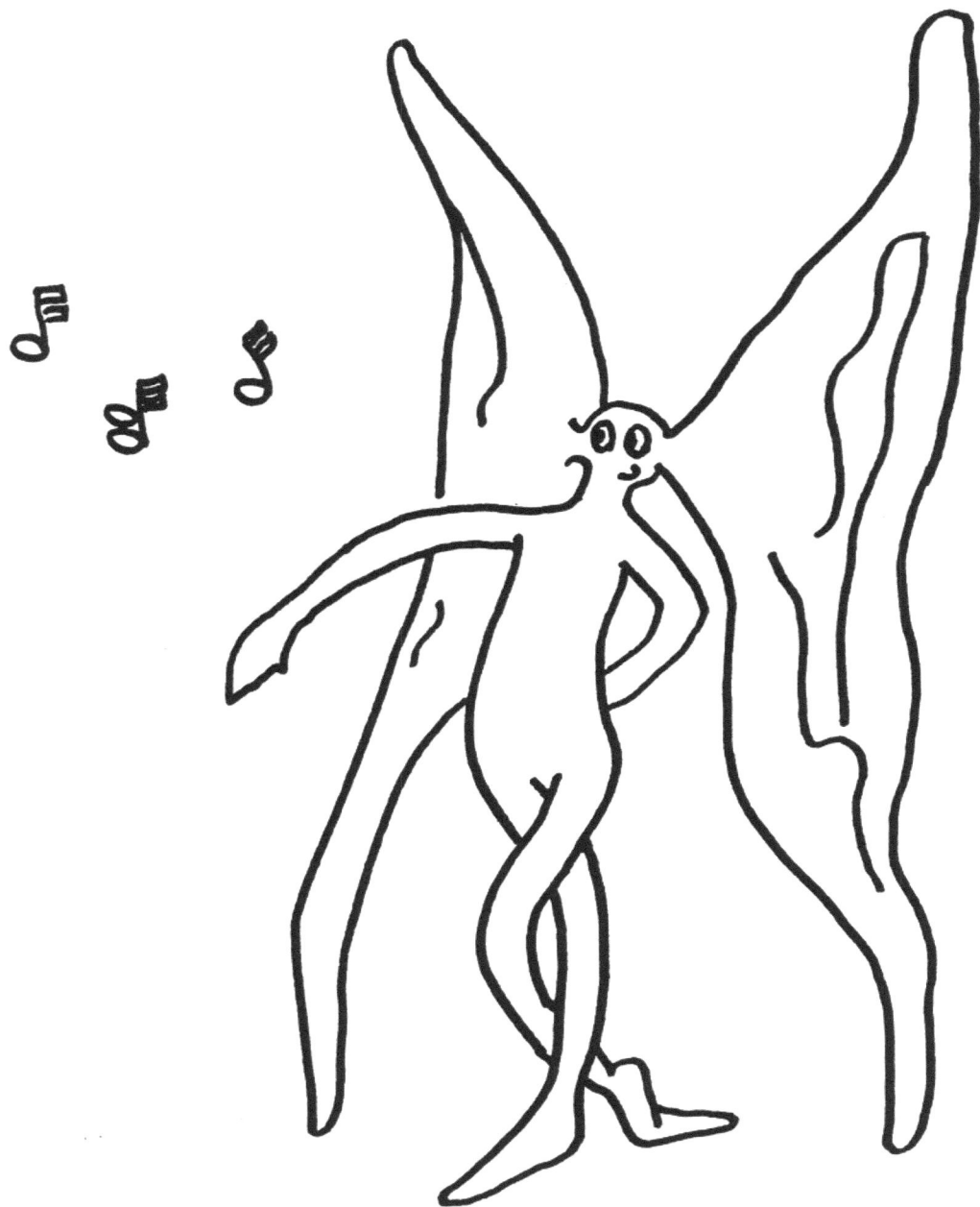

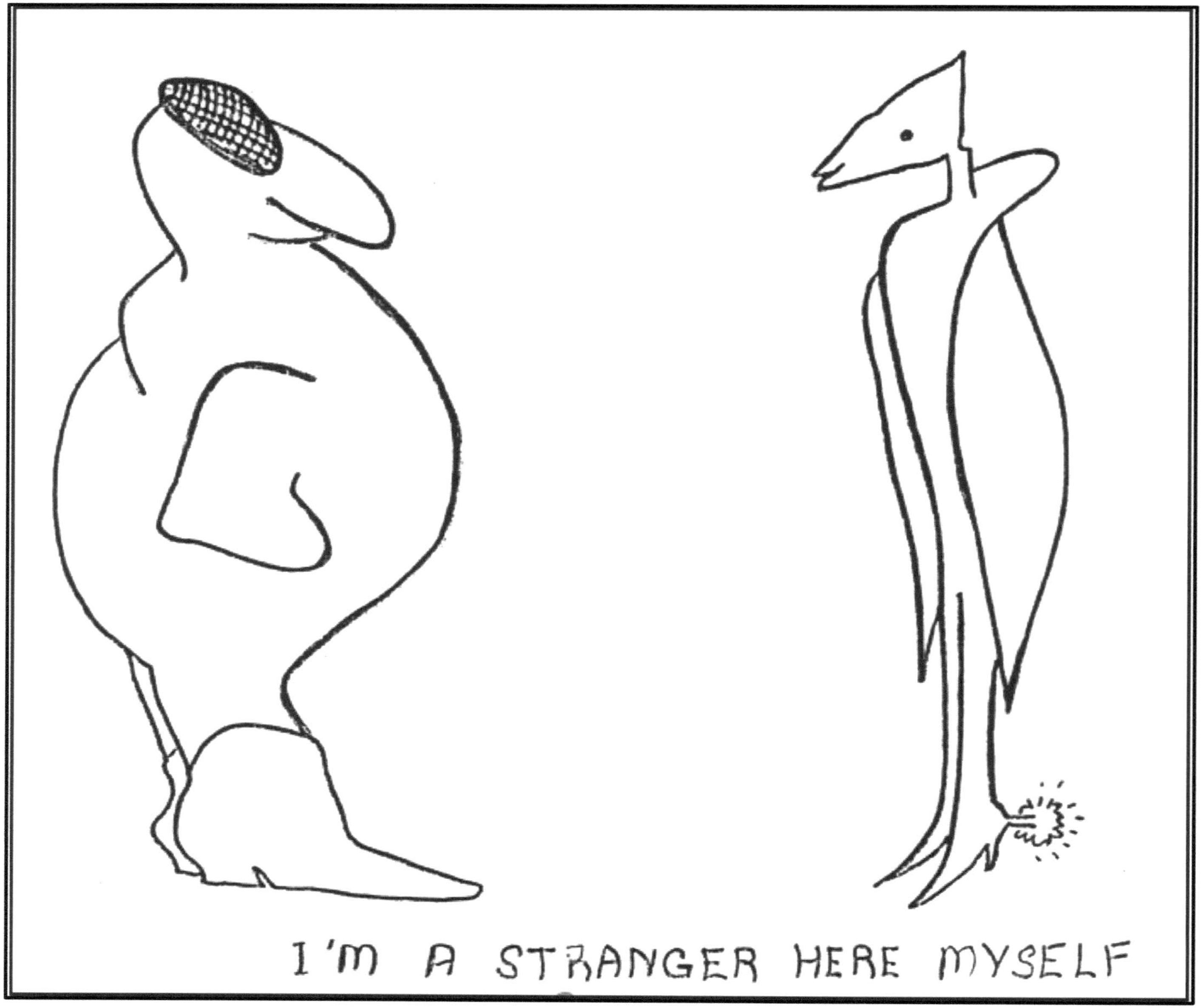

I'M A STRANGER HERE MYSELF

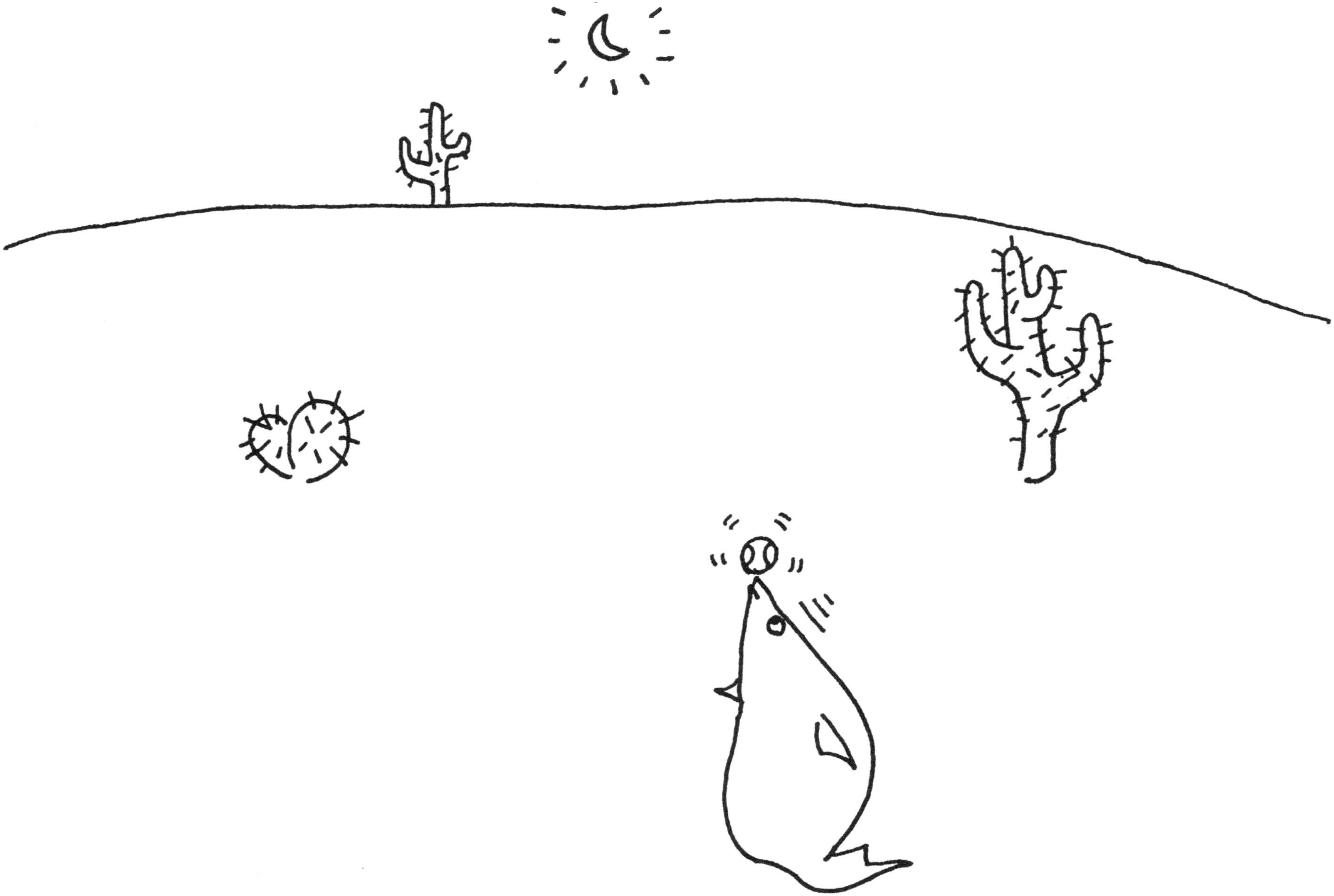

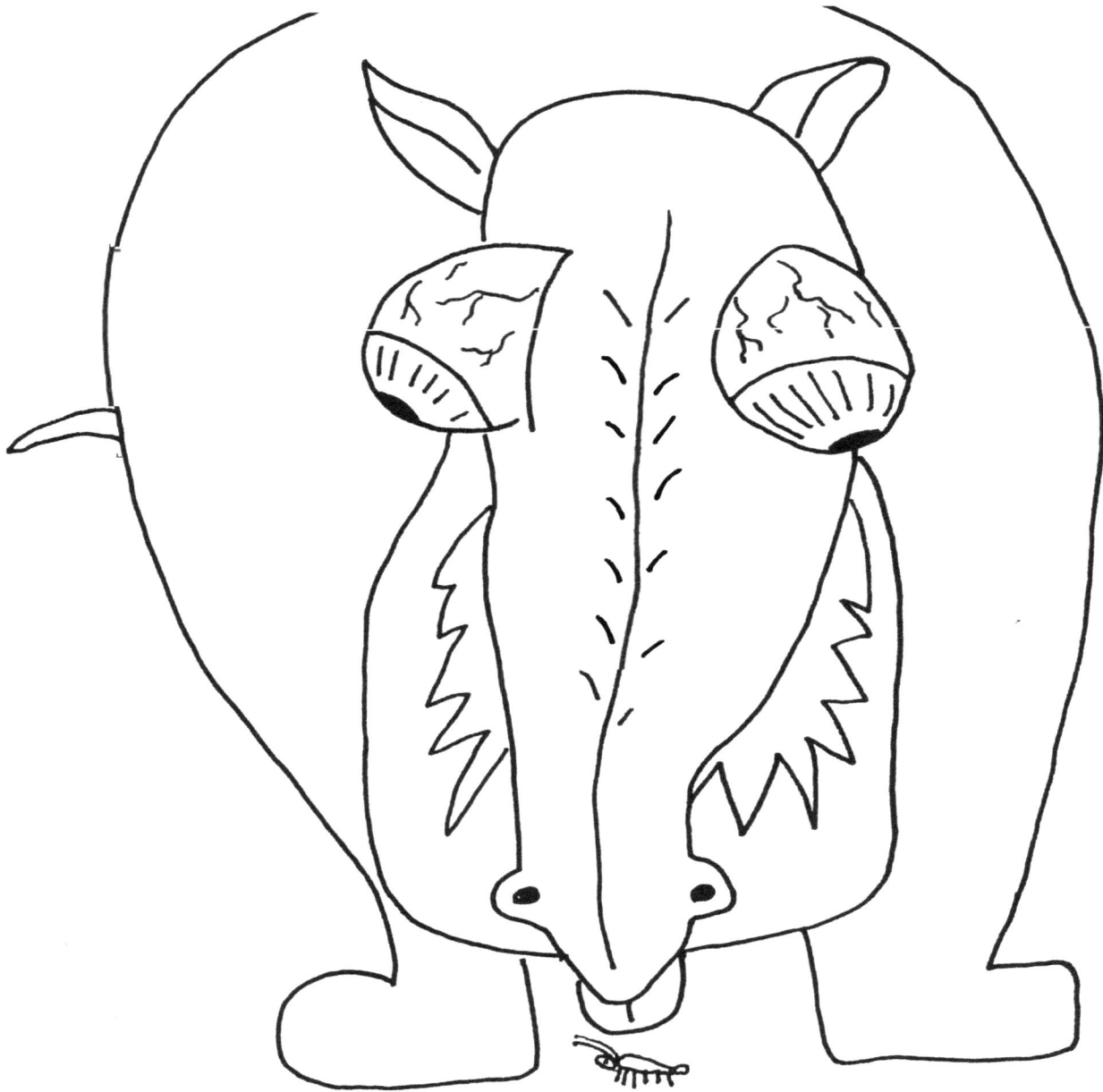

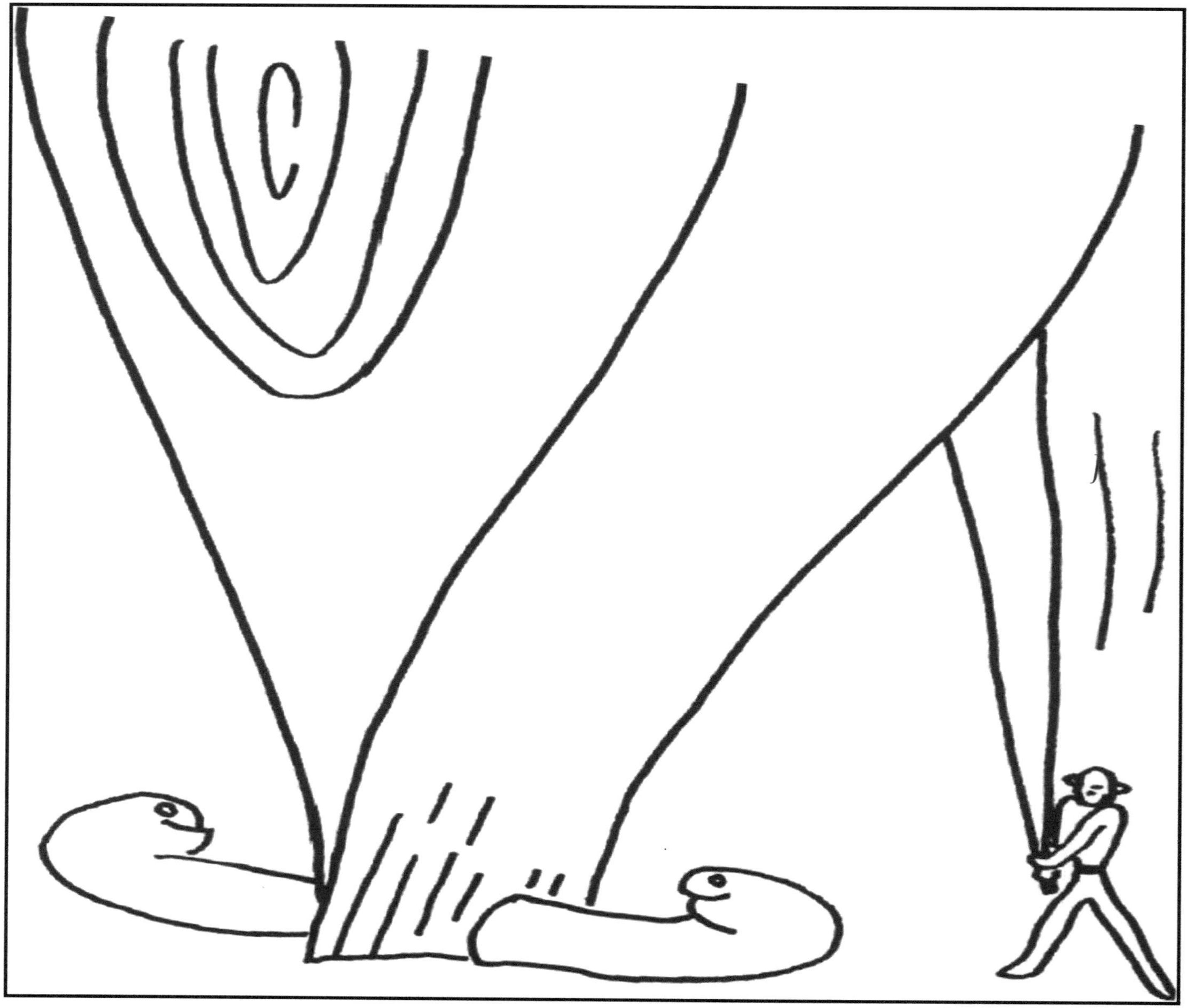

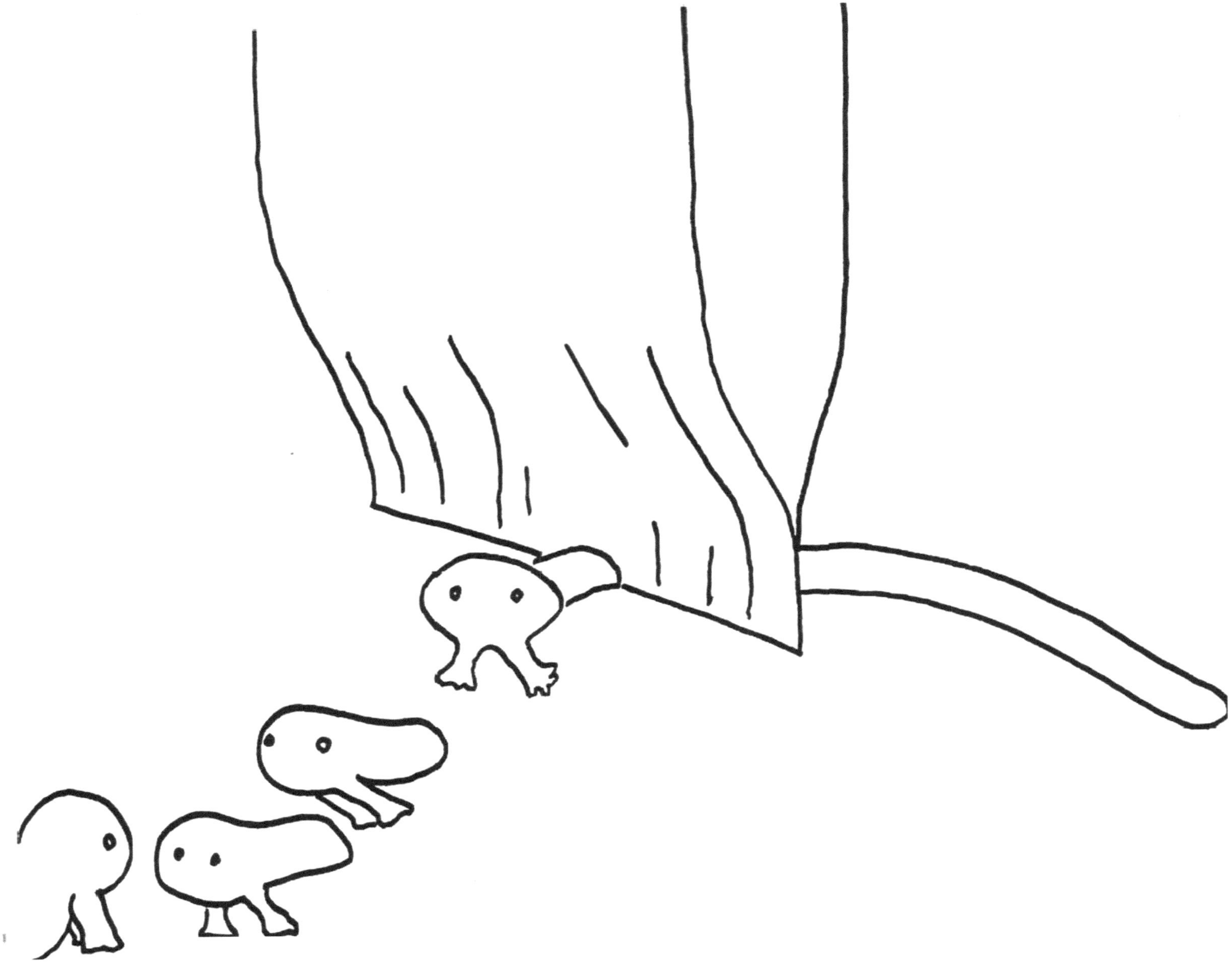

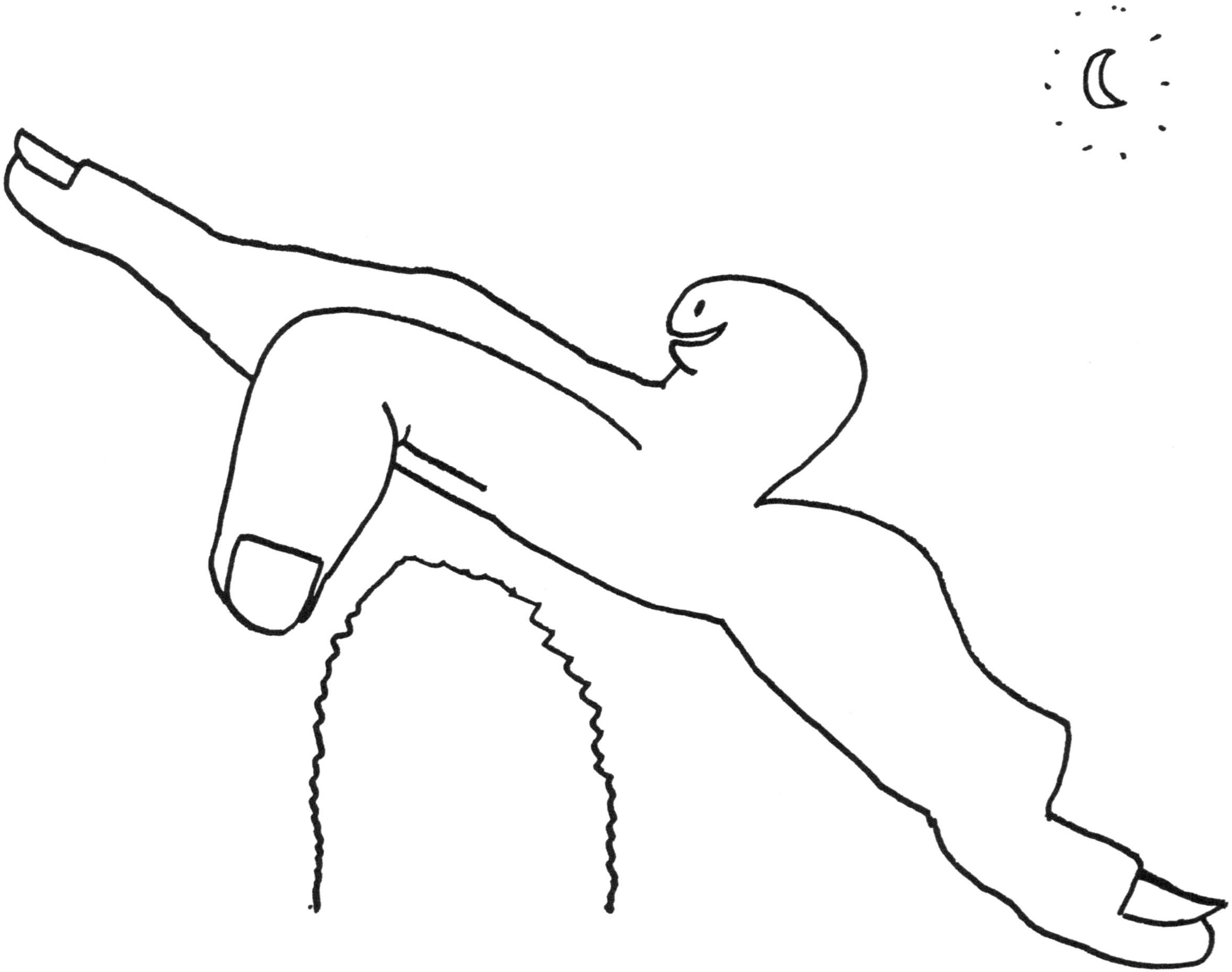

THREE-TOED HEDGEHOPPER

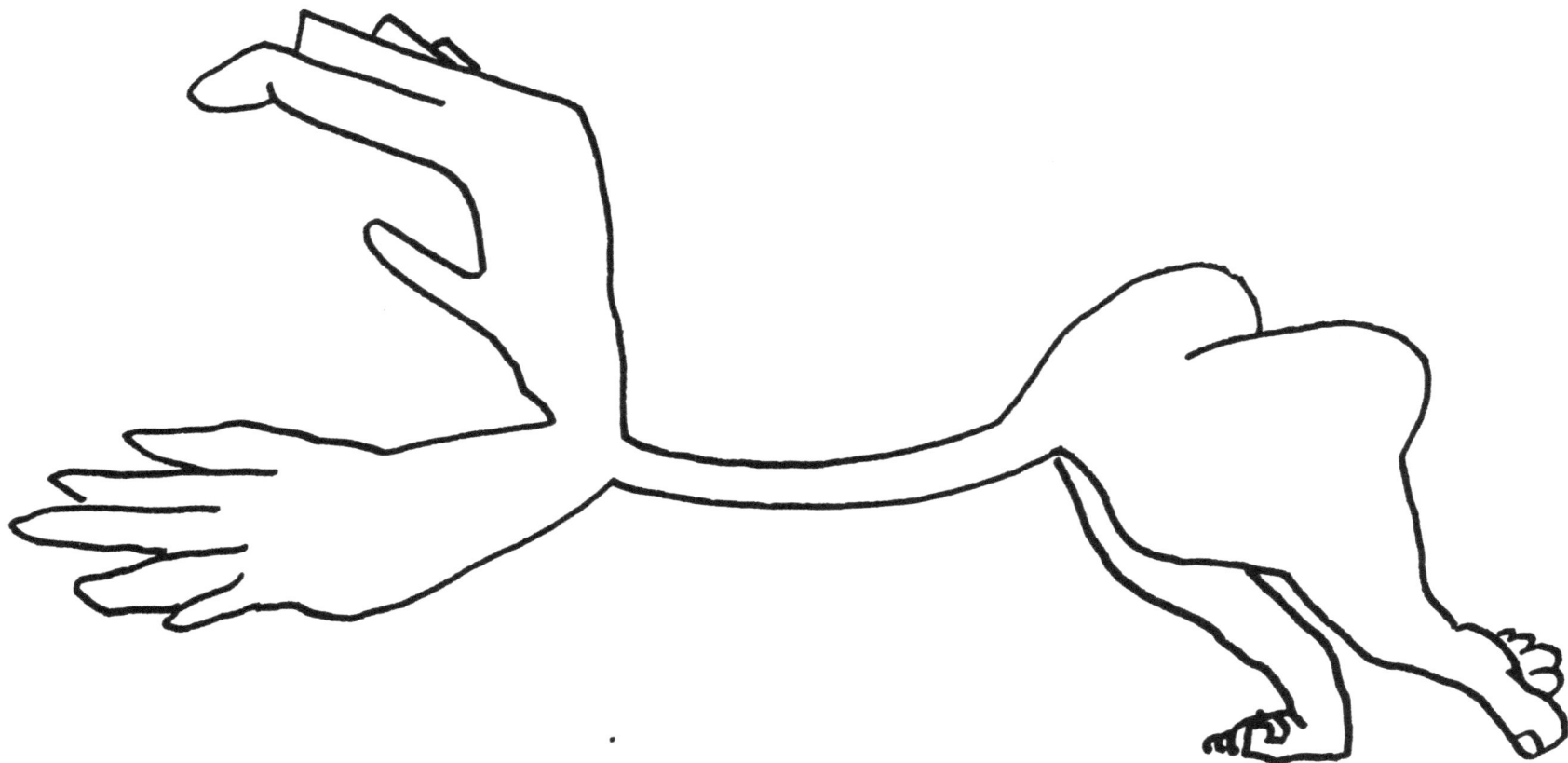

THE TWO-HANDED FOOTLOOSE

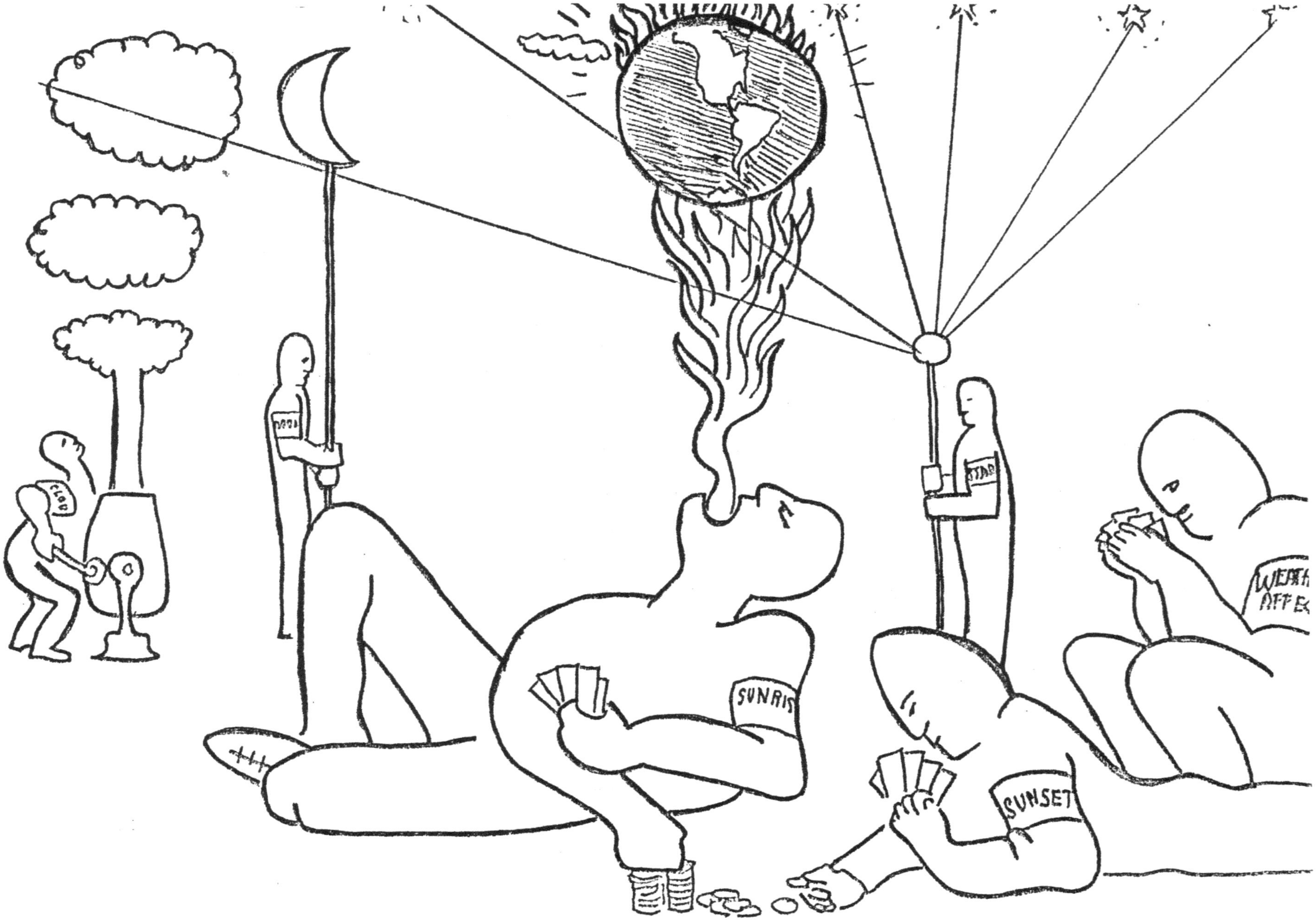
STAR
SUNRIS
SUNSET
WEATH
AFFEC

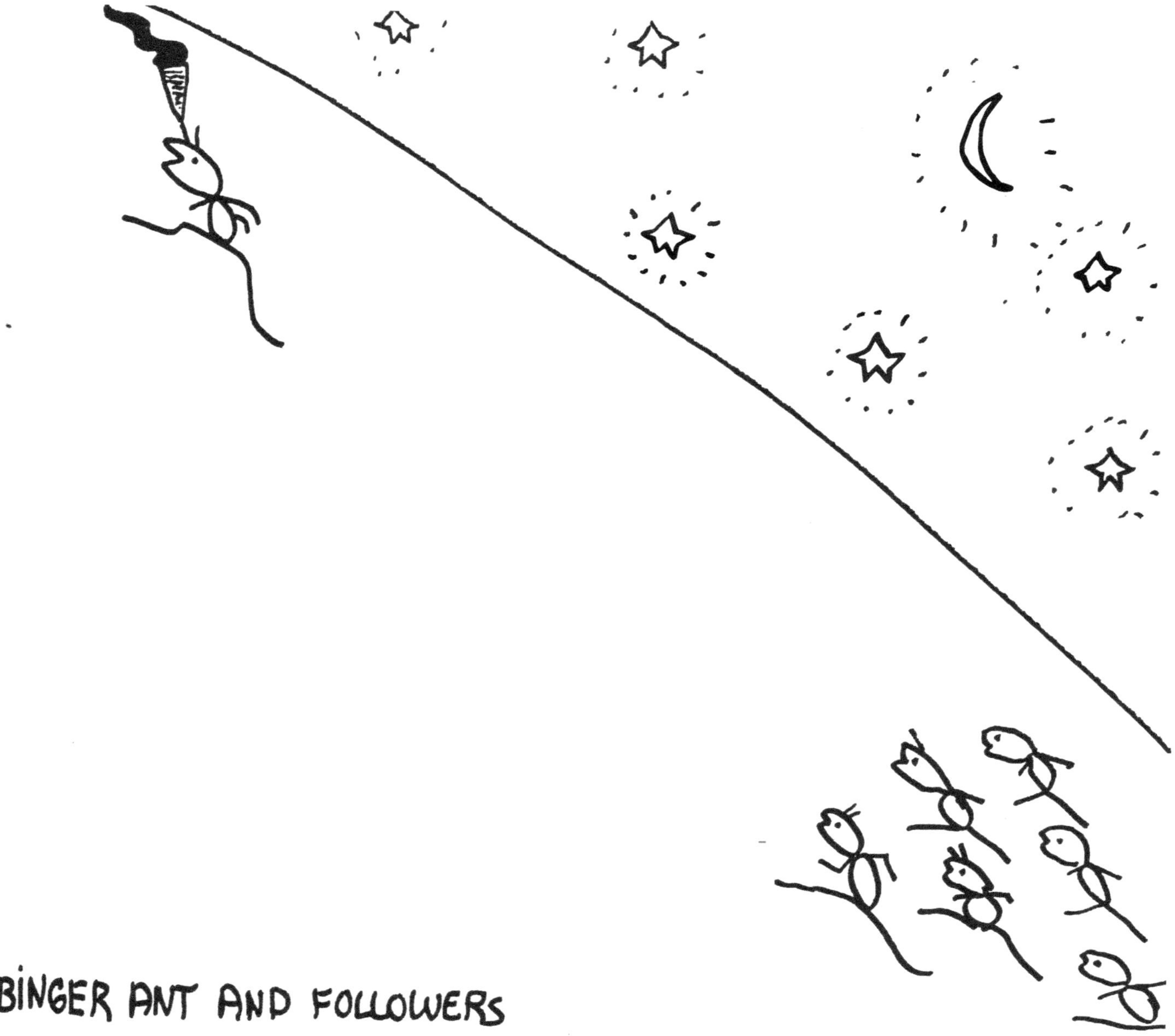

HARBINGER ANT AND FOLLOWERS

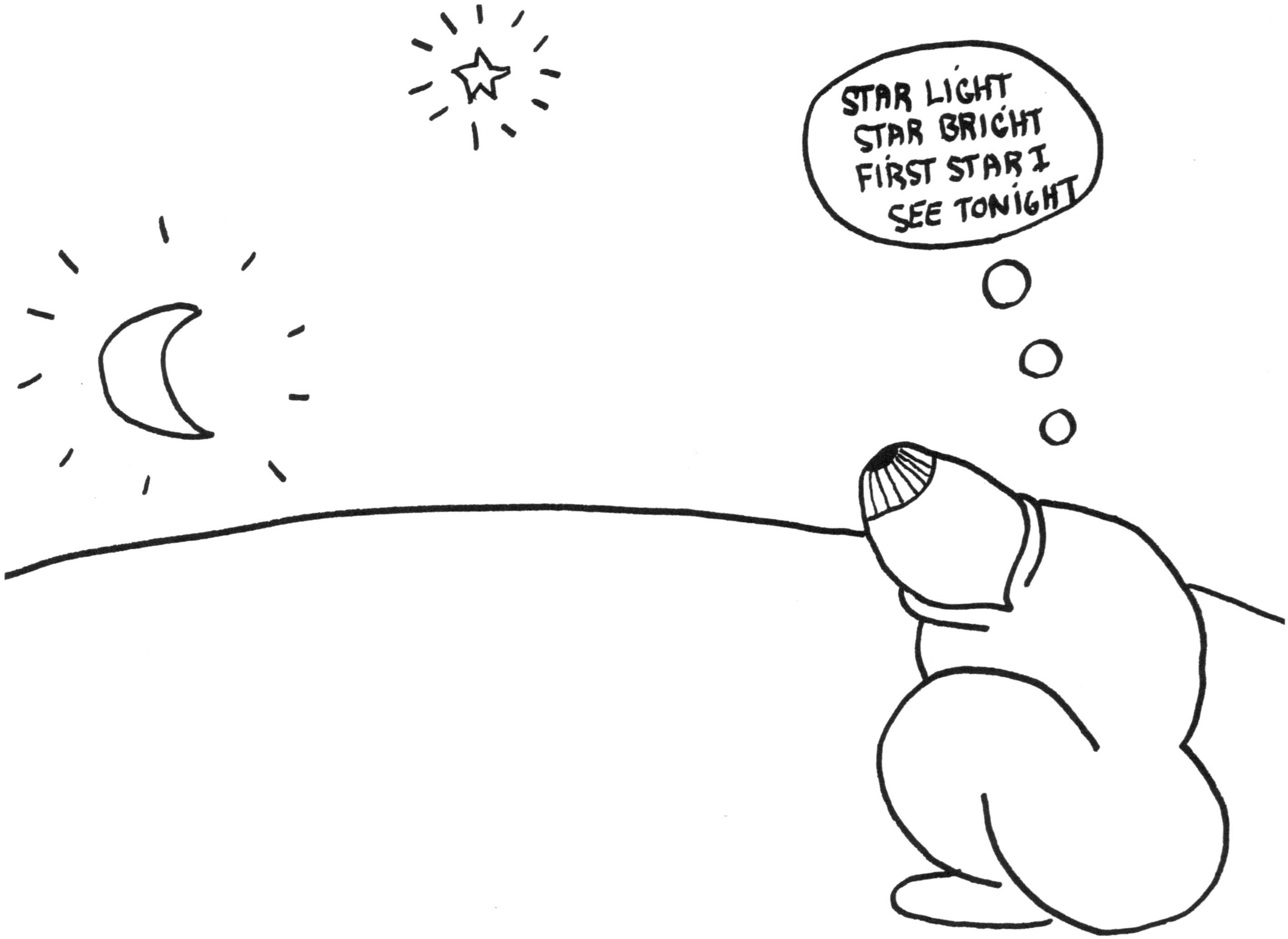
STAR LIGHT
STAR BRIGHT
FIRST STAR I
SEE TONIGHT

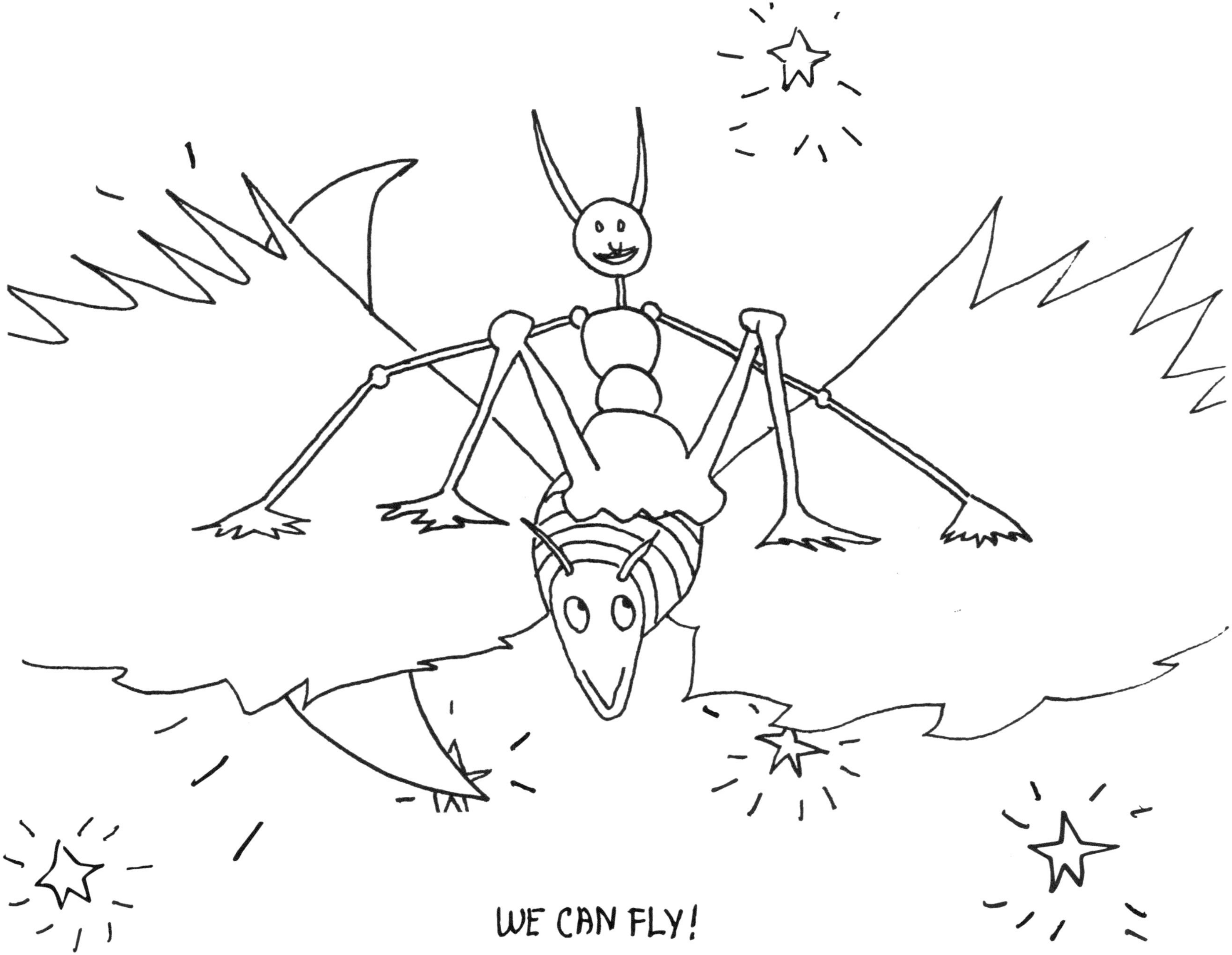

WE CAN FLY!

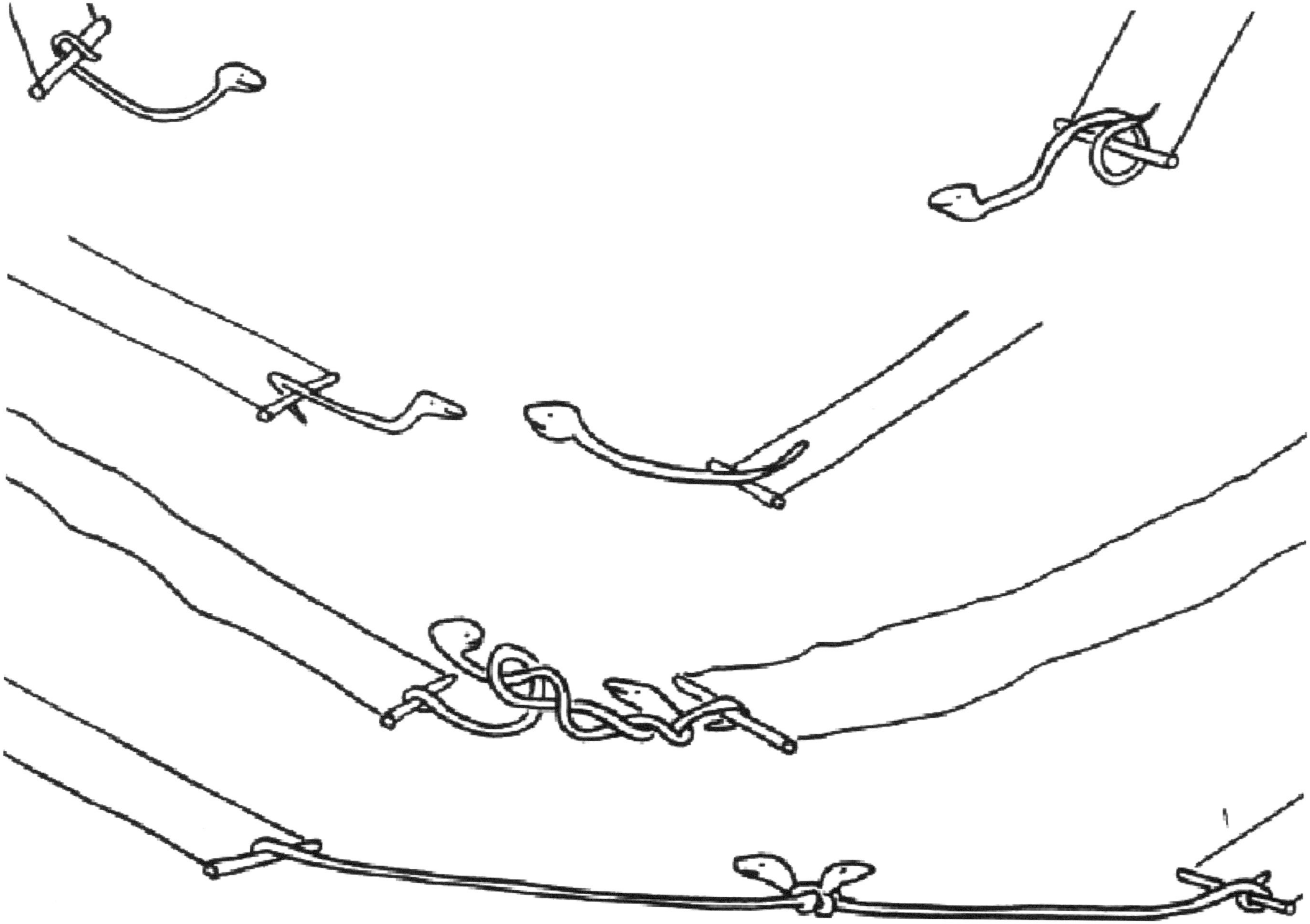

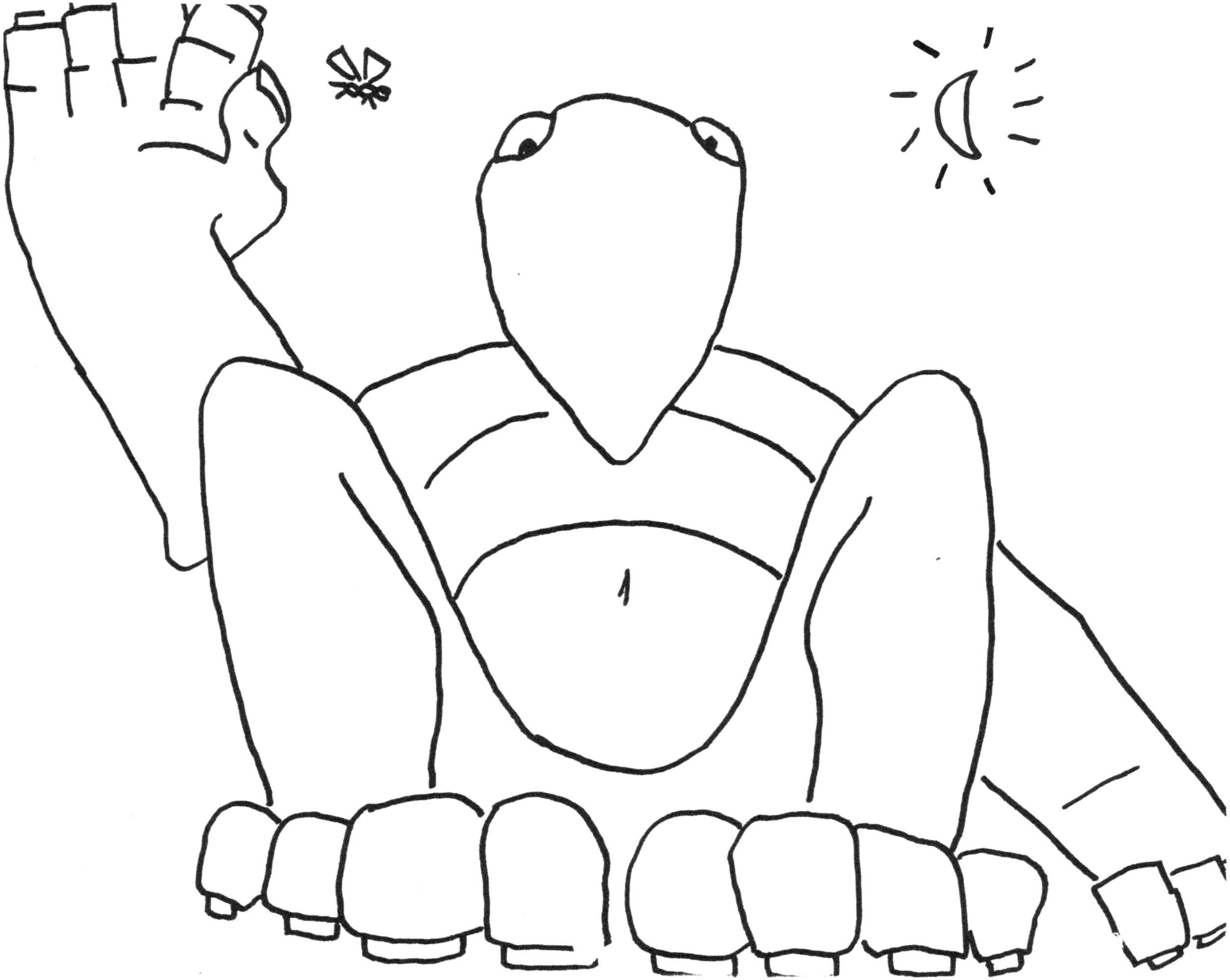

ALSO BY THE AUTHOR

Emanations from the Penumbra (poetry)
Malum in Se (stories)
Eclectica Americana (poetry)
Dates and Dreams, Prose Poems
Words in Passing (poetry)
Last Exit to East Hampton, Prose Poems
Resurgius, a Sixties Sex Comedy
Stories, Etc.
Manhattan Spleen, Prose Poems
A Portable Chaos, Rev. Ed. (novel)
The Ideologues (poetry)
The Journey and Related Poems
Reflections in a Doubtful I (poetry)
Carbons, a Career in Letters
Fortune Island (novel)
Time and Fevers (poetry)
A Fable & Other Prose Poems
Scenario for Scorsese (novel)
Paradise Square (novel)
Murderer's Day (poetry)
50 Poems
The Poor Boy and Other Poems

www.ingramcontent.com/pod-product-compliance
Lightning Source LLC
Chambersburg PA
CBHW040710150426

42811CB00061B/1811